Letts**Guide**

75ç

The South-west Peninsula Coast Path

3 Plymouth *to* Poole

Second edition

D1742750

by Ken Ward and John H N Mason

Charles Letts & Company Ltd,
London, Edinburgh, München and New York

Contents

First published 1977 by
Charles Letts and Company Limited
Diary House, Borough Road, London SE1 1DW
Second edition 1980
Cover and design: Ed Perera
Maps: Ian Ward
Cover photograph: J Allan Cash

© Ken Ward and John H N Mason
ISBN 0 85097 260 4

Printed in Great Britain by
Charles Letts (Scotland) Ltd

Introduction
Book 3 180 Miles of Coastal Walking

The South-west Peninsula Coast Path is unique; a walk of 500 miles through some of the finest coastal scenery in Europe.

Starting unpretentiously in a passage-way off Minehead Harbour it strides across the rich cliff tops of Somerset and North Devon, scrambles over the rocky shores and beetling cliffs of Cornwall, meanders through the sailing and holiday centres of South Devon and, after crossing the airy cliffs of Hardy country, finishes among the sand hills of Studland.

It is a rich tapestry this coastline, offering to the walker a variety of terrain unsurpassed by any of the other long-distance paths. Some of it is as challenging (and exhausting) as anything to be found on the Pennine Way or on the Fells. The ascent to the bare windswept summit of the Great Hangman which looms 1000ft above the boiling seas below or the scramble to the airy top of Houns-tout cliff with its eagle eye prospect of the Dorset coast should be enough to tempt the most ardent devotee of the Fells. Again, some of it would tempt the seaside holidaymaker into exploring.

The distinct advantage that the Coastal Path has over the Northern paths is the temperate climate of the South-west, which extends the walking period to late winter and early spring —in two years of out-of-season walking we counted wet days on the fingers of one hand.

Cornwall in the early spring is a dream: lonely cliffs and empty beaches, riots of daffodil and rhododendron, and long evenings to be spent sampling the local ale and gossip.

There is much else to distract and absorb the walker on this Coast. The peoples of this distinctive part of Britain have turned their hands to many pursuits in the cause of survival. The delightful fishing harbours remain as a tribute to the hardy generations of pilchard and mackerel fishers. The gaunt empty engine houses of the tin mines which stand sentinel on the Cornish cliffs provide a melancholy reminder of the industry's meteoric rise and fall.

The naturalist has a particular treat in store. The cliffs and sands are rich in flora and wildlife that have been driven from inland pastures by intensive modern agriculture. Its role as front line defence of the island has left this coastline rich in reminders of invasions that never came, striking an incongruous note in a harmonious and tranquil scene.

Although originally mooted some twenty years ago the path remains very much in a development state. Certain sections have been impeccably waymarked and cleared, other stretches are unmarked and overgrown. In producing this series of guides we have sought to provide the prospective walker with sufficient information and guidance to enable him to find even the most neglected paths.

How to use the Book

Walking the path

In some places the path is clearly signposted and easily followed, notably in National Trust areas. In others it may be less well marked and maintained but with the guide you should always find the route. The recommended path is shown as a solid green line. Alternatives are shown as broken lines.

Italics are used in the text to denote diversions from the walk itself, for instance comments on places of interest.

The sketch maps

The sketch maps are in no way designed to supplant the excellent series of Ordnance Survey Maps (1 : 50,000) and the walker is strongly recommended to provide himself with these. Appropriate reference numbers of the OS Maps are included in the diagrams on pages 6 and 7.

Distances

On the right-hand side of the maps an indication of approximate mileage is given.

Half-day walks or treks of several days

In preparing this guide we have sought to cater for everyone with an interest in the Path. Accordingly, with the guide, it is possible for the more serious walkers to spend a week or fortnight walking continuously. Equally it is possible for those whose interest extends only to an afternoon stroll to use the guide to select an appropriate stretch. To help in this we have included on the maps the most convenient access points to the Path, usually with adjacent car parking facilities.

Bus services Many are seasonal and others irregular. Always check locally. Bus time-tables are a help. Western National, Queen Street, Exeter (0392) 74191 will tell you which you need.

Refreshments Many refreshment places are only open June–August.

Bathing Often dangerous, particularly for non-swimmers. Be guided by flags and lifeguards.

Accommodation

The accommodation shown in the guide has been selected for its position close to the Path and capacity to provide overnight bed and breakfast.

Most have become known to the authors in the two years of walking and research that have gone into producing this guide, and we offer them in good faith without accepting responsibility for them. Some are excellent, some provide a reasonable service.

We have divided the accommodation into two price categories. The higher price range is indicated by a bed with knobs on. However when making reservations always check the costs.

No addresses are given but the information should be enough for postal location. Telephone numbers are given in every case so that you can call and ask for directions. As far as possible we have tried to indicate on the maps their approximate position in relation to the path. We recommend that you decide each evening your target for the following day and then book the nearest suitable accommodation to it. If they are full, ask them to suggest an alternative; you will find them all most helpful. Always check the price; always make clear whether or not you require an evening meal; and try to give some indication of the expected time of your arrival.

Two letters after the name indicate the period that accommodation is available, eg AO = April to October, SM = September to March, ie winter only. □ indicates that the place is open throughout the year including the winter months. However this is subject to, as one host put it, 'our week's holiday, the annual paint and spring clean and burst pipes!'

Other books in this series

This book covers the sector from Plymouth to Poole Harbour. The other two books in the series cover Minehead to St Ives (No 1) and from St Ives to Plymouth (No 2).

Index to Sections

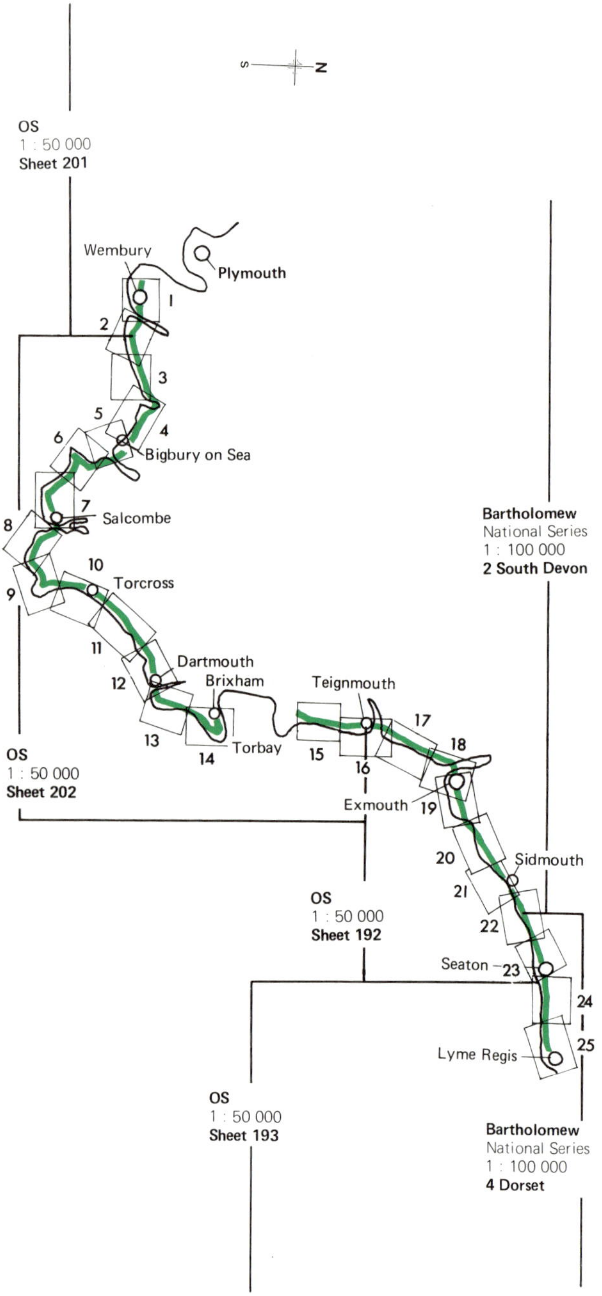

OS
1 : 50 000
Sheet 201

Wembury
Plymouth

2
1
3
5
4
6
Bigbury on Sea

7
Salcombe
8

10
Torcross
9

11
Dartmouth
12
Brixham
Teignmouth
13
Torbay
14

Bartholomew
National Series
1 : 100 000
2 South Devon

15
16
17
18
19
Exmouth

20
Sidmouth
21
22

Seaton 23
24
25
Lyme Regis

OS
1 : 50 000
Sheet 202

OS
1 : 50 000
Sheet 192

OS
1 : 50 000
Sheet 193

Bartholomew
National Series
1 : 100 000
4 Dorset

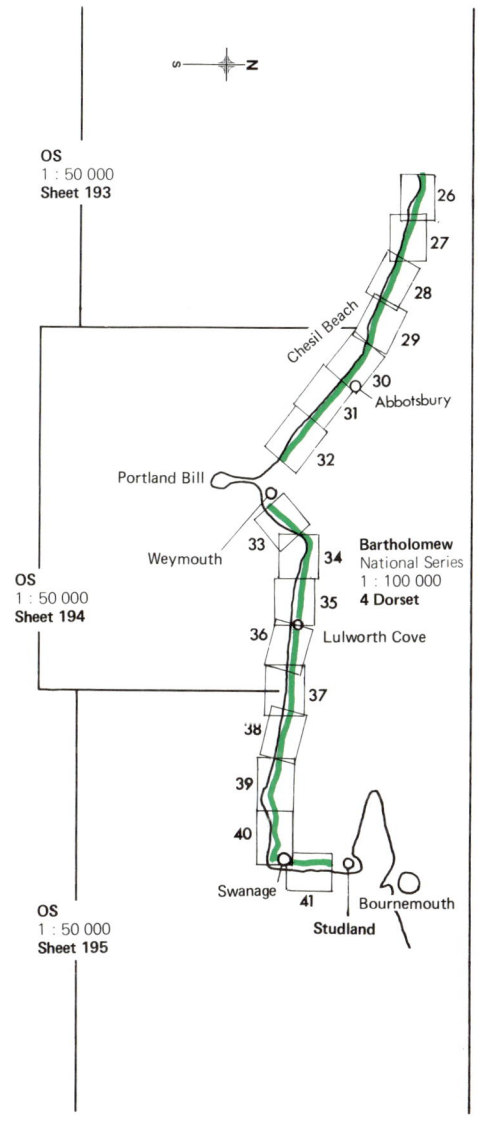

OS
1 : 50 000
Sheet 193

OS
1 : 50 000
Sheet 194

OS
1 : 50 000
Sheet 195

S —✦— Z

26
27
28
29
30
31
32

Chesil Beach

Abbotsbury

Portland Bill

Weymouth

33
34
35
36
37
38
39
40
41

Bartholomew
National Series
1 : 100 000
4 Dorset

Lulworth Cove

Swanage

Studland

Bournemouth

7

Tides

When walking the South-west Peninsula Coast Path a knowledge of the state of the tide on a particular day is often useful. On a stretch covered by this book you have to wade an estuary and this can only be done at low tide.

The table given below will enable you, with the help of your newspaper, to determine the approximate time of high and low water. You may also be able to buy local tide tables at newsagents.

Most national daily papers give the time of high water at London Bridge (usually with the weather details). By adding or subtracting the average time difference in hours and minutes given in the following table you can calculate the time of high water at the places mentioned. For intermediate places the time will be at some time between the two places each side. Low water is approximately 6 hours after high water.

		hrs	mins
Plymouth	Add	3	54
Salcombe	Add	4	05
Dartmouth	Add	4	28
Brixham	Add	4	31
Torquay	Add	4	35
Teignmouth (Approaches)	Add	4	32
Exmouth (Approaches)	Add	4	40
Lyme Regis	Add	4	50
Bridport	Add	4	32
Portland (Weymouth)	Add	5	05
Lulworth Cove	Add	4	55
Swanage	Subtract	5	18
Bournemouth	Subtract	5	08

Tidal predictions given above are computed by the Institute of Oceanographic Sciences, copyright reserved.

Pub Opening Times

Pub opening times can vary from district to district and from town to town and it is impossible to give information that applies everywhere. The following should however serve as a general guide to places on this sector of the Coast Path.

Mondays-Saturdays	**10.30-14.30**
	17.30-22.30*
Sundays	**12.00-14.00**
	19.00-22.30

*Usually open until 23.00 on Fridays and Saturdays, and on other weekdays from June-September.

Symbols

Symbol	Description
◇	Access to path
—	Path
▪▪▪	Alternative
---▷	Other footpaths
▶	Steeply up
▷	Steeply down
++++	Fence
∞∞∞∞	Hedge or wall
S	Stream
,G,	Gorse
,B,	Bracken
)(	Footbridge
⌂	Rocks near path
⬒	Paving stones
△	'Trig' point
NT	National Trust
CG	Coast Guard
▨	Shingle or sand
⬡	Rocks or boulders
⬛	Good beach
⬥	Swimming
⬥	Surfing
⬛	Lighthouse
▨	Incline
☆	Feature (see text)
Ⓟ	Parking
Ⓣ	Toilets
☎	Telephone
⬛	Shop
✕	Meals
☕	Light Refreshments
🍺	Pub
🍺	Pub specially recommended
🛏	Bed and breakfast lower to medium price range
🛏	Bed and breakfast more expensive
(all)	all above facilities
YH	Youth Hostel
□	Open all year
⛺	Camp site
△	Overnight pitch if permission obtained
⛪	Church with tower
⛪	Church with spire
Ⓕ	Ferry
🚂	Railway Station
🚌	Bus station
🚏	Bus stop
🌸	Birds or flowers

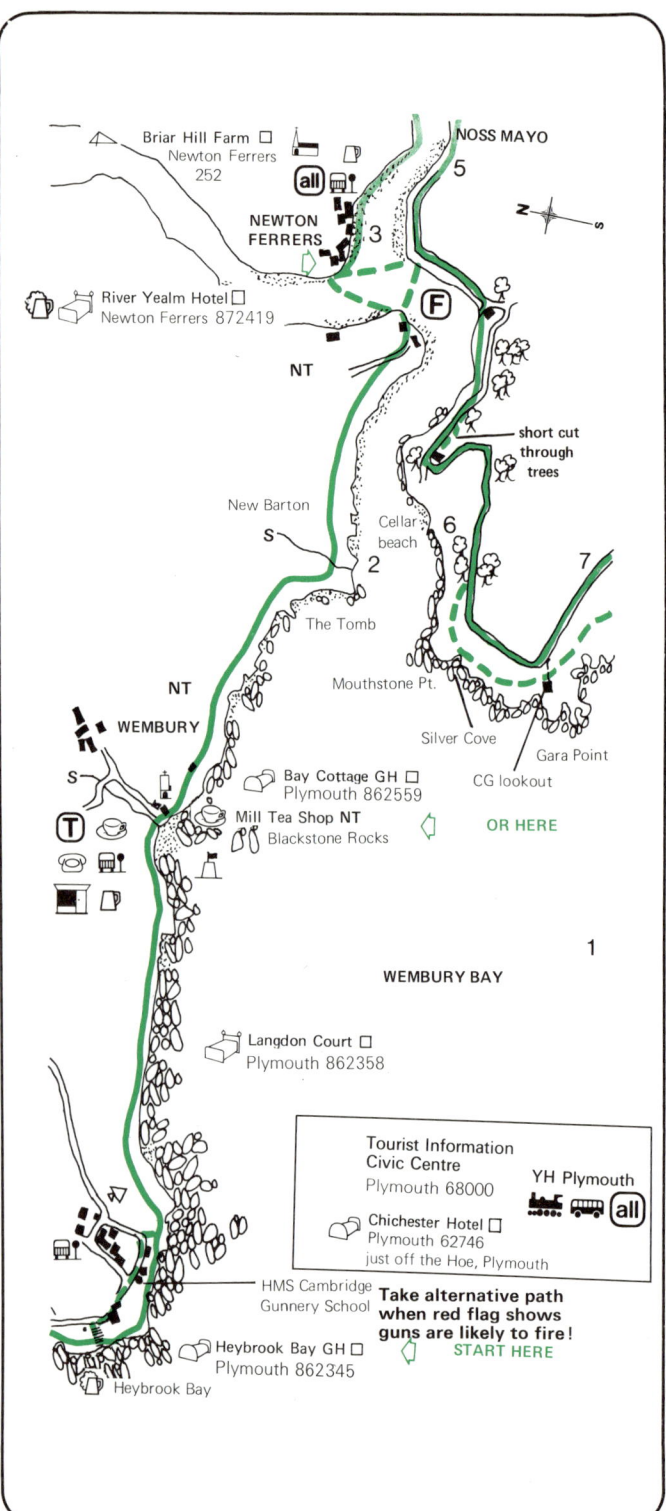

Briar Hill Farm ☐
Newton Ferrers
252

all

NOSS MAYO

5

NEWTON
FERRERS

3

River Yealm Hotel ☐
Newton Ferrers 872419

Ⓕ

NT

short cut
through
trees

New Barton

Cellar
beach

6

7

S

2

The Tomb

Mouthstone Pt.

NT

WEMBURY

Silver Cove

Gara Point

S

CG lookout

Ⓣ

Bay Cottage GH ☐
Plymouth 862559

Mill Tea Shop **NT**
Blackstone Rocks

OR HERE

1

WEMBURY BAY

Langdon Court ☐
Plymouth 862358

Tourist Information
Civic Centre
Plymouth 68000

YH Plymouth

all

Chichester Hotel ☐
Plymouth 62746
just off the Hoe, Plymouth

HMS Cambridge
Gunnery School

**Take alternative path
when red flag shows
guns are likely to fire!**

START HERE

Heybrook Bay GH ☐
Plymouth 862345

Heybrook Bay

10

1 Wembury (Plymouth)-Newton Ferrers-Gara Point

7 miles 11¼km From Plymouth 10¾* miles 17¼km

Joining the Coast Path: the official coast path begins at Turnchapel on Plymouth Sound but initially this involves a great deal of road-walking through built-up areas. We therefore recommend that in the Summer months you begin your walk either at Wembury Beach (No. 64 bus from Plymouth) or at Heybrook Bay (No. 61 bus). From October to April we suggest you start at Newton Ferrers or Noss Mayo (No. 94 bus). This is because less than 2 miles from Wembury there is the River Yealm which can only be crossed by ferry May to September. For those walking to or from Cornwall—see Book 2 *From St Ives to Plymouth*—the Cremyll passenger ferry runs to and from Admiral's Head, a short street at the end of which there is a bus service connecting with the city centre.

Going: from Wembury Beach to Newton Ferrers and beyond is fine open country. Newton Ferrers is a most attractive sailing centre (see below *re* Yealm ferry). At Wembury is a pleasant sandy beach and a National Trust centre in an old mill-house where refreshments are served. Note that once you leave Newton Ferrers there are no refreshment facilities for the next 15 miles, apart from the little shop and café at Stoke, open only in the summer.

On a hillock above Wembury Beach is the 15th-century church with its 14th-century tower, a prominent landmark for mariners. Up the road from the beach is the Old Wheel pub, and a substantial built-up area of villas, etc. There is, however, little accommodation to be had.

The Path continues through pleasant cliff-top National Trust land, largely pasture.

The ferry across the Yealm to Newton Ferrers only runs in the summer May/September; the last one is 17.30. If you are on the west bank of the river, shout for attention. It is advisable to phone beforehand to the ferry operators (0752) 872210.

Newton Ferrers has its older houses at the head of the estuary. The church is mainly 15th century with some parts 13th century. Noss Mayo, another attractive hamlet of mediaeval origins, is joined to Newton Ferrers. Pubs: Dolphin, Beacon Hill at Newton Ferrers; Swan and Old Ship at Noss Mayo.

The ferry may be taken across to Newton Ferrers (River Yealm Hotel) with a long, but attractive walk around the estuary, or you may ferry directly across to the road that leaves Noss Mayo. This is the coastal path. The road becomes a wide path, climbing higher past former Coast-Guard cottages, emerging in open country above Gara Point, with fine views back along the Cornish coast and ahead towards Prawle Point.

* From Turnchapel via Heybrook Bay.

11

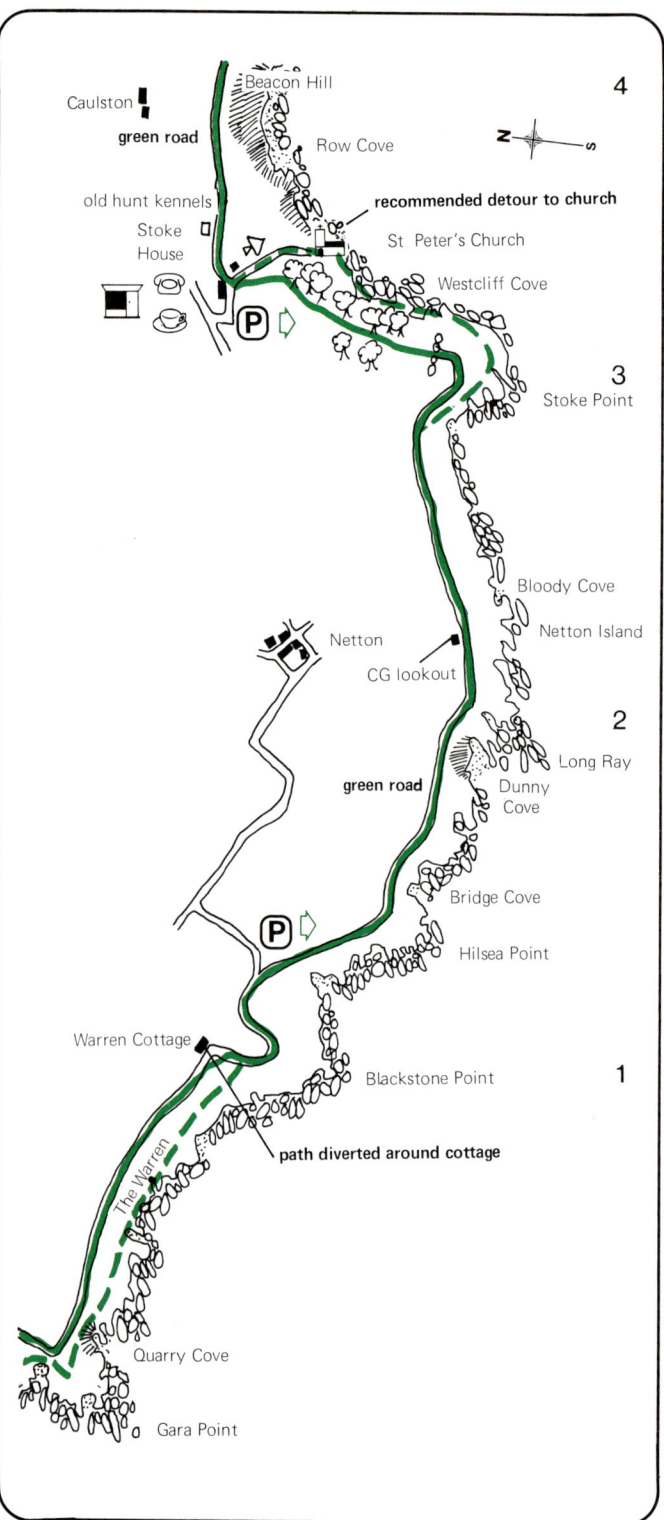

Caulston

green road

old hunt kennels

Stoke
House

P

Beacon Hill

Row Cove

recommended detour to church

St Peter's Church

Westcliff Cove

3
Stoke Point

Bloody Cove

Netton Island

Netton

CG lookout

2

Long Ray

Dunny
Cove

green road

Bridge Cove

Hilsea Point

P

Warren Cottage

path diverted around cottage

Blackstone Point

1

The Warren

Quarry Cove

Gara Point

4

N — S

2 Gara Point-Beacon Hill

4 miles 6½km   From Plymouth 14¾ miles 23¾km

Going: pleasant cliff-top walking without any difficulty.

On the next section, Beacon Hill-Erme Mouth-Beacon Point, you have to cross the Erme Estuary, with no ferry or bridge. The only method is to wade and this is only possible at low tide. You will need to take this into consideration when planning your walk. Hints on how to find the time of high and low tide are given on page 8.

The Path continues as a wide track round Gara Point, along the 200ft cliff top with wide sea views, past the lone Warren Cottage. Seals and porpoises are to be seen in the summer. The countryside inland is quite unspoiled and empty of human habitation except for a farmhouse or two. After rounding Stoke Point the Path passes through a pleasing patch of woodland, coming out at a road junction and a small cluster of houses around Stoke House. In one of these houses you can get refreshments in the summer.

Approaching Stoke Point a diversion can be made on the seaward side by a footpath to the 14th-century St Peter's Chapel, the abandoned former parish church of Noss Mayo, nearly 2 miles from its village. The chapel is in the course of renovation. Here is another ancient church which could very well have been built to provide a guide to shipping. Look for the tombstone, reputed to be that of a pirate, on the floor in the south-east corner. Also the wall table to Miriam K Kingscombe who died on board a ship with a rather splendid name.

The Path can be regained by a steep road through a holiday site run by the Co-operative movement.

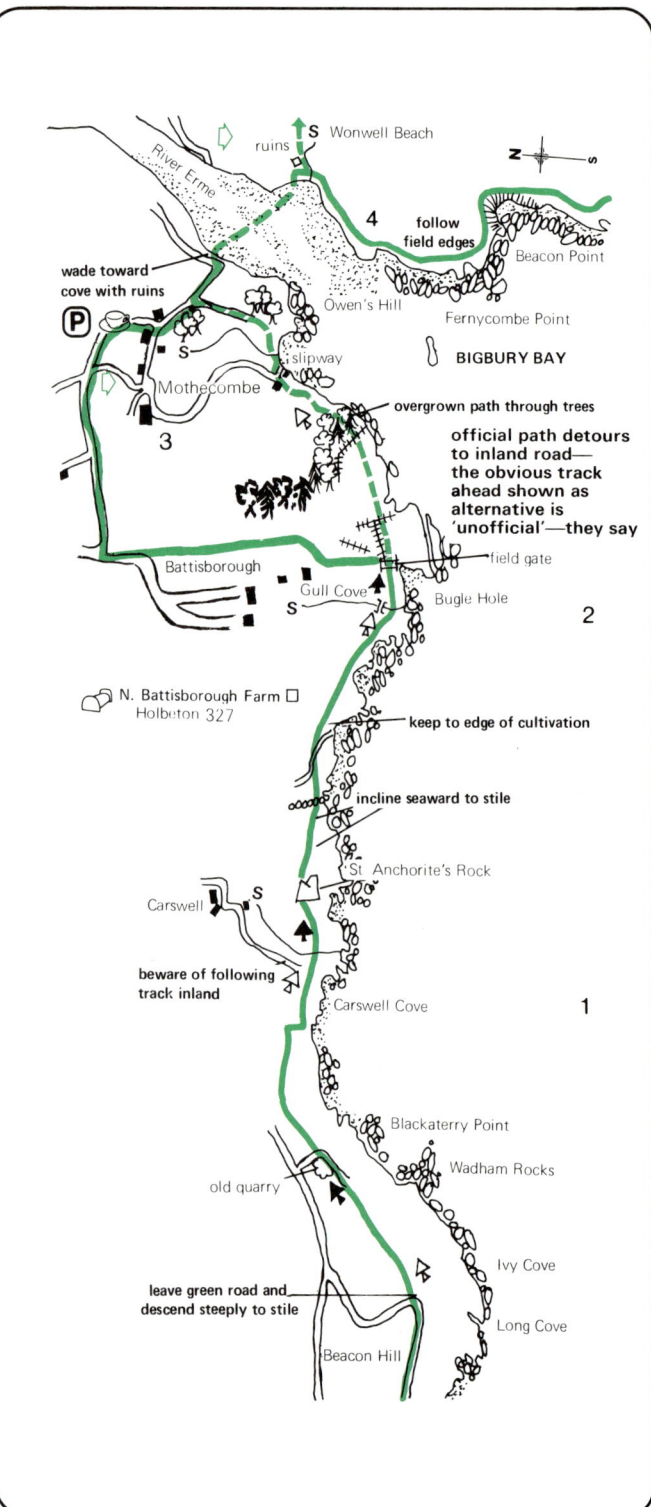

River Erme

ruins **S** Wonwell Beach

4 follow field edges

Beacon Point

wade toward cove with ruins

Owen's Hill

Fernycombe Point

(P)

s

Mothecombe

slipway

BIGBURY BAY

overgrown path through trees

official path detours to inland road— the obvious track ahead shown as alternative is 'unofficial'—they say

3

Battisborough

field gate

Gull Cove

s

Bugle Hole

2

N. Battisborough Farm ☐
Holbeton 327

keep to edge of cultivation

incline seaward to stile

St Anchorite's Rock

Carswell

s

beware of following track inland

Carswell Cove

1

Blackaterry Point

Wadham Rocks

old quarry

leave green road and descend steeply to stile

Ivy Cove

Long Cove

Beacon Hill

3 Beacon Hill-Erme Mouth-Beacon Point

4¾ miles 7¾km   From Plymouth 19½ miles 31½km

Going: the crossing of the estuary of the river Erme is the problem here. There is no bridge nor ferry. For about an hour each side of low tide you should, however, be able to wade across. You have a strenuous 3 miles in front of you to Bigbury.

From Beacon Hill the track of the Path is clear and continues along the cliff-top, with one or two steepish slopes to negotiate, to St Anchorite's Rock and Bugle Hole. There is no path round the coast beyond Bugle Hole at present; the route turns inland, coming out on the road leading through Mothecombe and down to the river's edge.

The ford, at low tide, leads across to the road you will see opposite or you can make directly across towards Wonwell Beach with the ruined cottages (one was a pilot house, kept white as a mark for shipping). It should be possible to wade across the ford for about an hour each side of low tide (see page 8 for hints on how to find out the approximate times of high and low tide).

From the beach the Path climbs clearly, bordering agricultural land, following the cliff-edge, until the 300ft Beacon Point is rounded.

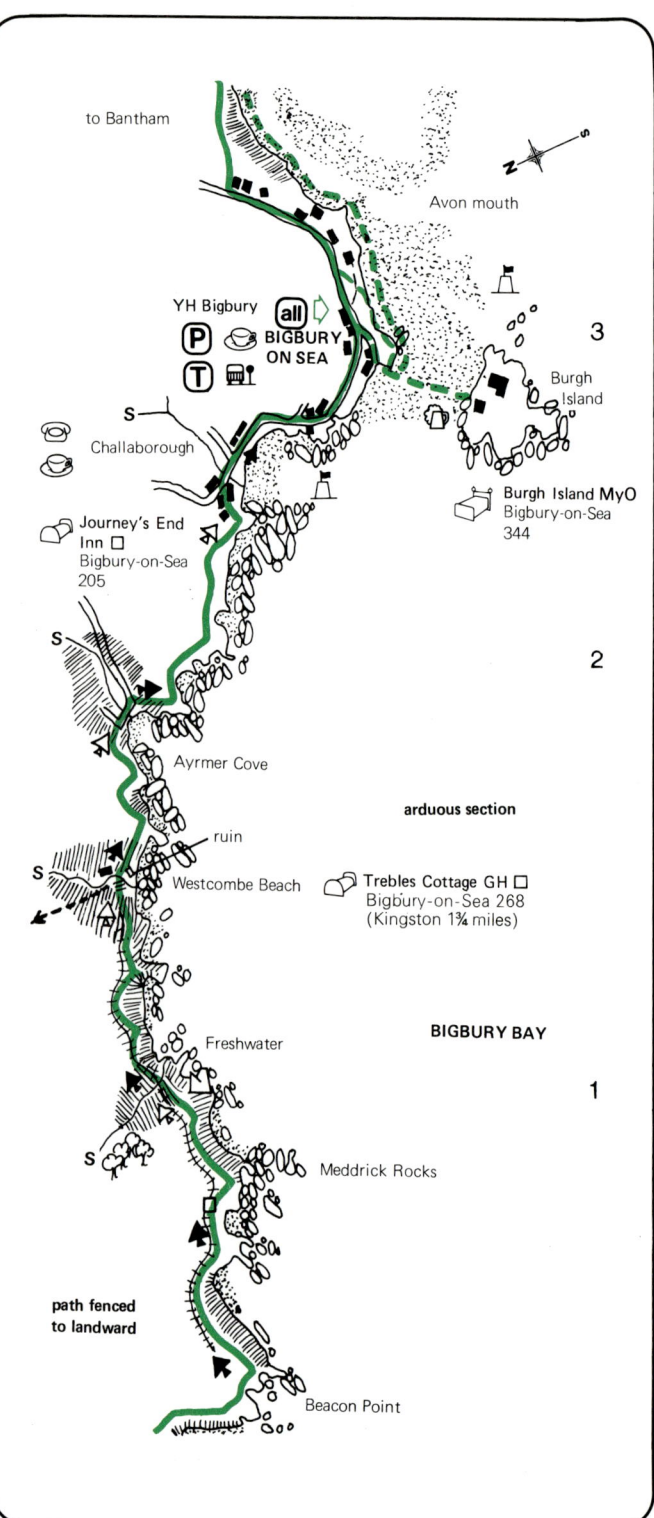

to Bantham

Avon mouth

YH Bigbury

P **(all)** ▷
☕ **BIGBURY
ON SEA**

T 🏛

S

☕ Challaborough
☕

Burgh
Island

🏠 Burgh Island MyO
Bigbury-on-Sea
344

🏠 Journey's End
Inn □
Bigbury-on-Sea
205

S

3

2

Ayrmer Cove

arduous section

ruin

S

Westcombe Beach

🏠 Trebles Cottage GH □
Bigbury-on-Sea 268
(Kingston 1¾ miles)

BIGBURY BAY

Freshwater

1

S

Meddrick Rocks

path fenced
to landward

Beacon Point

4 Beacon Point-Bigbury on Sea

$3\frac{3}{4}$ miles 6km From Plymouth $23\frac{1}{4}$ miles $37\frac{1}{2}$km

Going: some very steep gradients on the first two miles which might be beyond the capabilities of the elderly or inexperienced. The rest is straightforward.

From Beacon Point for almost two miles the Path runs as a narrow track between the boundary fence, unfortunately of barbed-wire, of the large Scobbiscombe estate and the cliff edge—very close to the edge in some places. There are some extremely steep gradients, particularly the one leading down to Westcombe Beach and up the other side, and these need careful negotiation especially in wet or windy weather.

There is a delightful pub The Journey's End, where Sheriff wrote his famous play, at Ringmore 1 mile inland from Ayrmer Cove, where accommodation is also available. The village itself is also of interest, with its 13th-century church.

Challaborough has a sandy beach but bathing can be dangerous at certain times. Bigbury on Sea, a bungalow resort, crowded in the summer, offers all the usual facilities to the visitor, including a Youth Hostel. Off Bigbury and connected by a sandy causeway is Burgh Island. In the Middle Ages there was a chapel to St Michael of which no trace remains. The only buildings now are the large hotel and a pub. At high tide a form of tractor on stilts (designed by a visitor) takes you across the 300yd causeway. The hotel, formerly a millionaire's home offers accommodation in flatlets and has a good restaurant. The hotel also runs the adjacent ancient pub, the Pilchard (1335), whose exterior and interior must have looked very much the same for hundreds of years.

You now have to cross the river Avon or Aune (pronounced Orne) from Bigbury to Bantham. At the time of writing there is a ferry running 9-21 April and 21 May-29 September: 10.00-11.00; 15.00-16.00 Monday-Saturday; also on Sundays in July and August. The ferry is operated from the fourth building opposite in Bantham, a thatched boathouse with 5 dormer windows, (H Cater, Thurlestone 593). Shout 'Ferry!' The best route (except at high tide) to the ferry point is to walk along the sands bordering the estuary. Otherwise the official route is along the busy main road out of Bigbury for about 1 mile, turning off down the footpath alongside the house Mount Folly. This will bring you to the sands on the bank of the river opposite the Bantham ferry point.

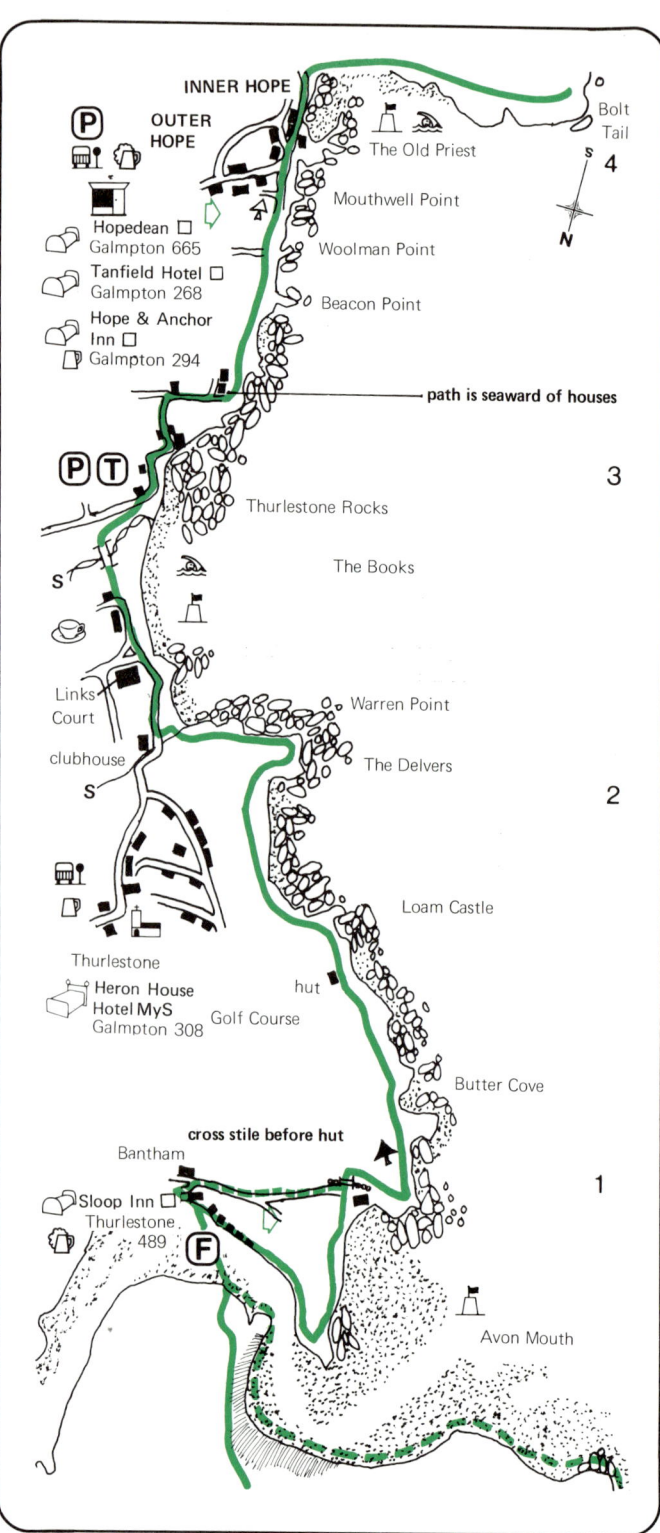

INNER HOPE

P

OUTER
HOPE

The Old Priest

Bolt
Tail

4

Mouthwell Point

Hopedean □
Galmpton 665

Woolman Point

Tanfield Hotel □
Galmpton 268

Beacon Point

Hope & Anchor
Inn □
Galmpton 294

path is seaward of houses

P **T**

3

Thurlestone Rocks

The Books

S

Links
Court

Warren Point

clubhouse

The Delvers

S

2

Loam Castle

Thurlestone

Heron House
Hotel MyS
Galmpton 308

hut

Golf Course

Butter Cove

cross stile before hut

Bantham

Sloop Inn □
Thurlestone
489

F

1

Avon Mouth

5 Bantham-Thurlestone-Hope-Bolt Tail

4¾ miles 7¾km. From Plymouth 28 miles 45¼km

Going: the Path on this section involves no difficulties or need for great effort. You are beginning to approach the parts of Devon which are very popular in the summer and small resorts are likely to be crowded.

Once safely across the Avon river you have two pubs at Bantham: the mediaeval Sloop, also providing accommodation, and the Old Ship which has a restaurant.

The sandhills and sandy shore at Bantham attract a number of motorists and their families in the summer. The Path runs parallel to the bank of the estuary and then turns south-east to follow the coast, running along the seaward boundary of the Thurlestone Golf Course for 1¼ miles. A short diversion is made round the block of flats, Links Court, to avoid a cliff fall.

Thurlestone (derived from Old English meaning 'pierced stone', from the arched rock on the shore) is another popular destination for holidaymakers with excellent sands and safe bathing. The old village is 1 mile inland. A long footbridge takes you over marshy ground where there is a nature reserve.

As there are houses right up to the edge of the cliff the Path follows the road inland for a few yards, then it turns to the right and climbs along the edge of the cliff. You soon arrive high above the much-photographed twin villages of Inner and Outer Hope, the old part huddled round the sandy Hope Cove. In the high season you can hardly move for motor coaches and crowds. A quiet and beautiful spot is the Square in Inner Hope, just behind the street above the Cove.

The Path climbs quite steeply from the road in Inner Hope by the old Methodist Chapel to the impressive headland, Bolt Tail, with the clear imprint of an Iron Age cliff fort on the summit.

It was off Bolt Tail that the dreadful disaster overtook HMS Ramilles *in the winter of 1760 when it was wrecked with the loss of 800 lives. Only a few were saved.*

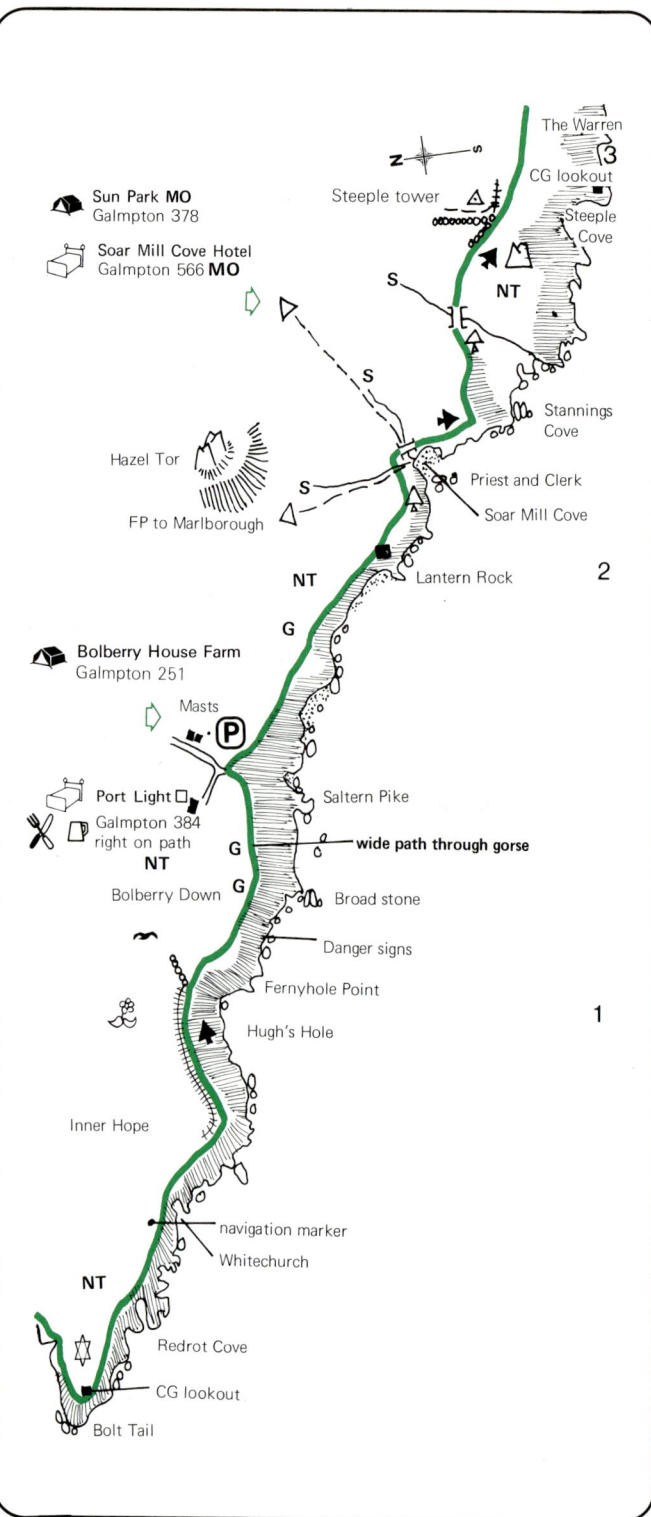

The Warren

CG lookout

Steeple tower

Sun Park **MO**
Galmpton 378

Soar Mill Cove Hotel
Galmpton 566 **MO**

Steeple
Cove

S

NT

Stannings
Cove

S

Priest and Clerk

Hazel Tor

S

Soar Mill Cove

FP to Marlborough

NT

Lantern Rock

2

G

Bolberry House Farm
Galmpton 251

Masts

P

Saltern Pike

Port Light

Galmpton 384
right on path

G

wide path through gorse

NT

G

Bolberry Down

Broad stone

Danger signs

Fernyhole Point

Hugh's Hole

1

Inner Hope

navigation marker

Whitechurch

NT

Redrot Cove

CG lookout

Bolt Tail

6 Bolt Tail-The Warren

3¼ miles 5¼km   From Plymouth 31¼ miles 50½km

Going: from Bolt Tail for 5 miles to Bolt Head probably the most spectacular high-cliff walking on the south coast. Steep gradients to overcome at Soar Mill Cove.

The Path follows the coastline high above the sea.

The massive rock formations for 10 miles from Bolt Tail to Prawle Point and for a few miles inland differ from those on either side. Known as metamorphosed mica schists, the original rocks have been transformed through gigantic pressures. The shining flakes of mica and white outcrops of quartz may be seen. Near the tall radio masts ahead on Bolberry Down (named after the nearby hamlet which is mentioned in the Domesday Book) is a road, serving a former wartime installation, which brings numbers of motorists to the cliffs in the summer. Refreshment facilities in the summer at the Port Light, by the radio masts.

The going becomes steep with the sharp descent to Soar Mill Cove with an equally exacting gradient up the other side. There are one or two paths to choose from but it can be a steep slope whichever you choose.

The whole area from just the other side of the Bolt Tail to Bolt Head is National Trust land, the longest stretch owned by the Trust. In their pamphlet they draw attention to the birds and wild flowers. Besides herring and greater black-backed gulls there are shags and fulmars to be seen on the cliffs in the early summer. There are also ravens and buzzards. Besides thrift, you can find the blue vernal squill.

Once past Soar Mill Cove the Path to Bolt Head via the Warren presents no difficulty.

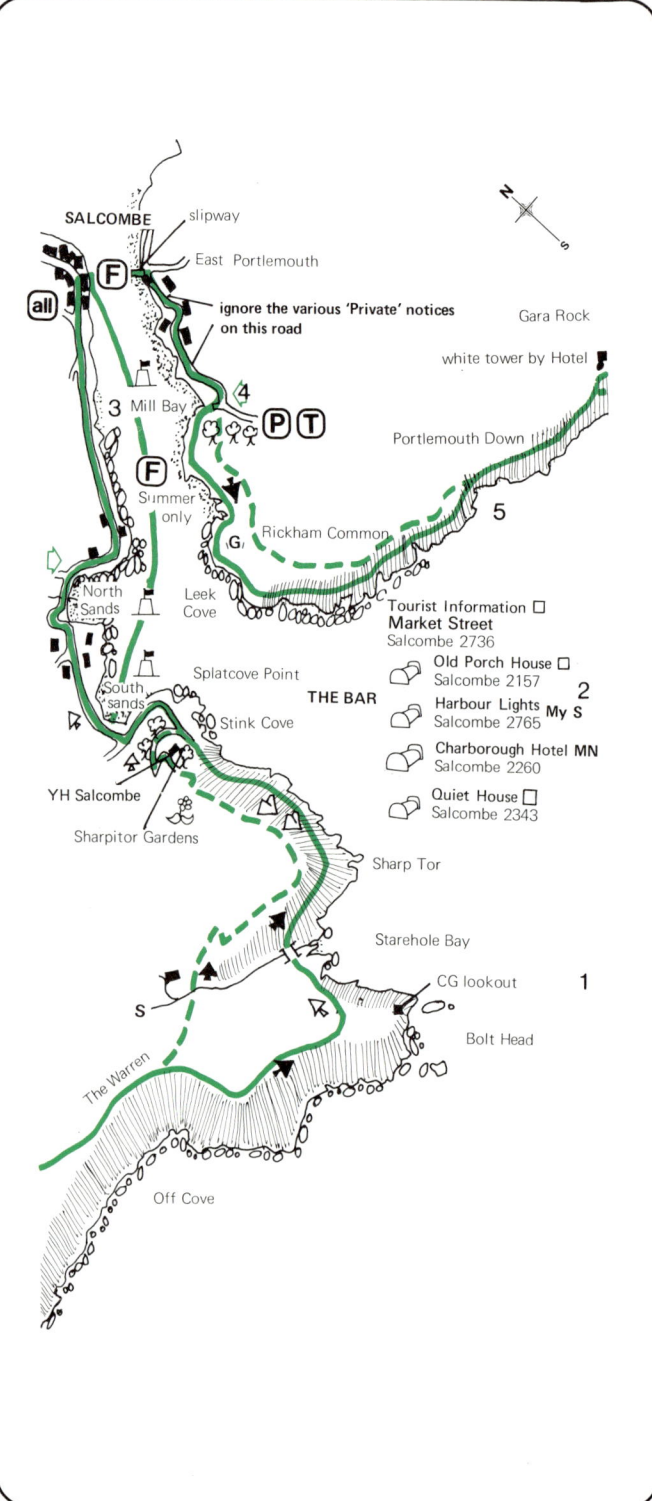

SALCOMBE
slipway
F
all
East Portlemouth
ignore the various 'Private' notices on this road
Gara Rock
white tower by Hotel
3 Mill Bay
4
P T
Portlemouth Down
F
Summer only
Rickham Common
5
G
North Sands
Leek Cove
Tourist Information □
Market Street
Salcombe 2736
Splatcove Point
THE BAR
Old Porch House □
Salcombe 2157
2
South sands
Stink Cove
Harbour Lights
Salcombe 2765
My S
YH Salcombe
Charborough Hotel MN
Salcombe 2260
Sharpitor Gardens
Quiet House □
Salcombe 2343
Sharp Tor
Starehole Bay
CG lookout
1
S
Bolt Head
The Warren
Off Cove

7 The Warren-Bolt Head-Salcombe-Gara Rock

5¾ miles 9¼km   From Plymouth 37 miles 59¾km

Going: after taking you up to Bolt Head the Path descends
gradually to Salcombe. Across the estuary begins another
rewarding cliff-top stretch.

Beyond the Warren there is more than one path which you
can take to Salcombe but the most attractive is that which
takes you along the cliff edge, (follow sign 'South Sands via
Bolt Head') up to Bolt Head and then down to Starehole Bay
until you join the beautiful paved Courtney Walk. Sharp left at
the end of the walk is Sharpitor Gardens, with museum and a
collection of rose plants and shrubs, and the Youth Hostel.
As you round the flank of the 400ft Sharp Tor you have a fine
view of Salcombe and the estuary. The road leads round to
the beaches of South Sands and North Sands. There is a ferry
in the summer (last one 18.00) from South Sands to the centre
of Salcombe.

If pressed for time there is a path inland via East Soar
farm and across fields.

*Salcombe (population 2500); Devon's most southerly
resort, enjoys an equable climate throughout the year. Until
150 years ago it was a small port whose importance was
restricted because of the sandy bar across the harbour mouth.
Tennyson is said to have been inspired to write his famous poem*
Crossing the Bar *while staying with Froude, the historian, in the
town. Salcombe is probably the largest yachting centre in
Britain, the estuary and its branches providing superb anchorage.
It is also well-known for its fishing. There are some delightful
buildings along Fore Street, the main street. The ruined
Salcombe Castle or Fort Charles was built by Henry VIII. It
was one of the last Cavalier strongholds to yield to the
Roundheads in Devon.*

The Ferry across the harbour to East Portlemouth runs
daily from Fore Street all through the year (last departure:
20.30 summer; 19.50 winter; one hour earlier on Sundays).

*The attractive village of East Portlemouth with its old
church was a rival to Salcombe in the Middle Ages. It sent
5 ships for Henry V's invasion fleet in the 14th century.*

The road leading seaward from the Ferry landing brings
you through woods to the small safe sandy beaches of Small's
Cove and Mill Bay. From Mill Bay the Coast Path is the
footpath nearest to the estuary shore; it continues through
woods and then over the gorse of Rickham Common, below
the cliff-top of Portlemouth Down to the slopes below the
prominent Gara Rock with its flagstaff.

Note: unless you make the detour inland to East Prawle
(section 8) there are no refreshment facilities in the 10 miles
between Gara Rock and Hallsands.

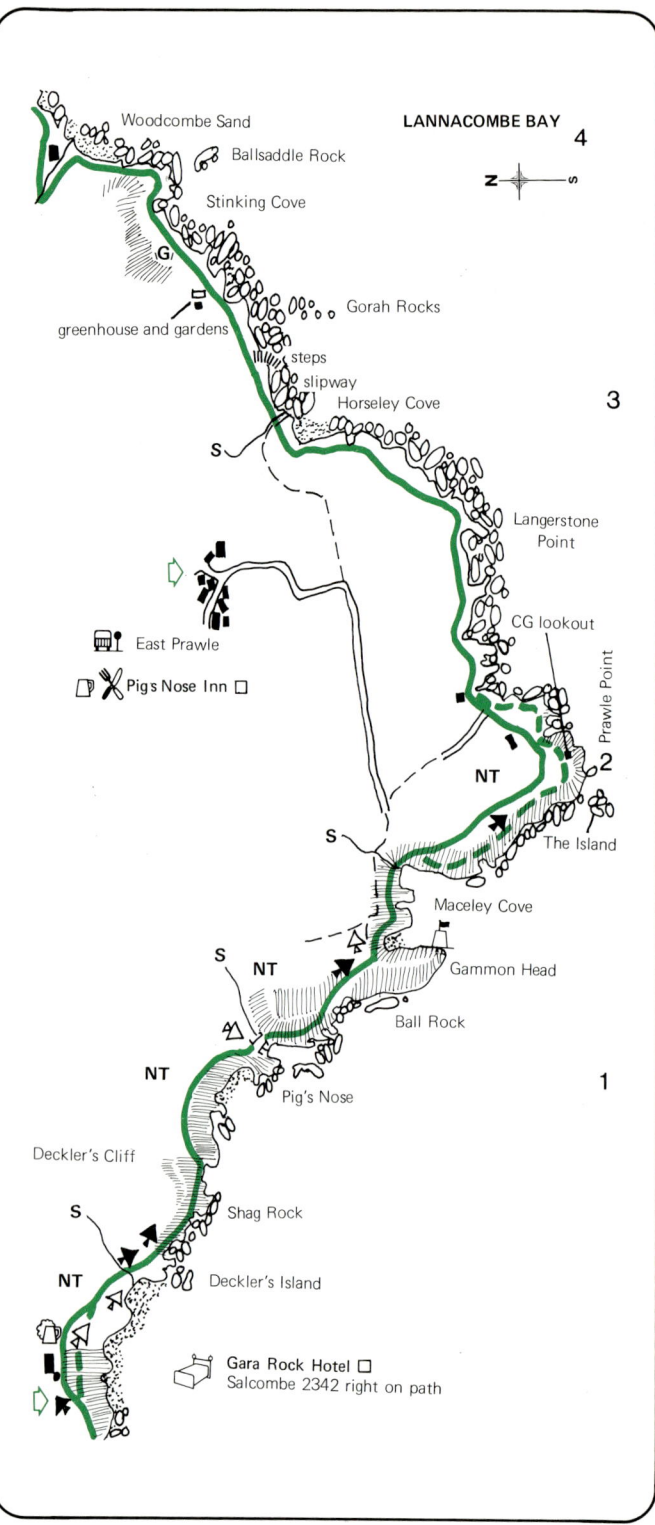

LANNACOMBE BAY

Woodcombe Sand

Ballsaddle Rock

Stinking Cove

Gorah Rocks

greenhouse and gardens

steps
slipway

Horseley Cove

Langerstone Point

CG lookout

Prawle Point

East Prawle

Pig's Nose Inn

NT

The Island

Maceley Cove

Gammon Head

Ball Rock

Pig's Nose

NT

Deckler's Cliff

Shag Rock

Deckler's Island

NT

Gara Rock Hotel
Salcombe 2342 right on path

N

8 Gara Rock-Prawle Point-Lannacombe Bay

$4\frac{1}{4}$ miles 7km   From Plymouth $40\frac{1}{4}$ miles $66\frac{3}{4}$ miles

Going: this continues the sector from Salcombe to Prawle
Point which we think is as satisfying as any on the south
Devon Path. Almost as spectacular as the Bolt Tail to Bolt
Head stretch, it is more lonely and wild mainly because road
access is limited. Steep gradients above Maceley Cove;
otherwise undulating but straightforward.

The Path continues through the bracken below the Gara
Rock Hotel (there is also a path up to the hotel) to just above
the small beach and then proceeds, through National Trust
land, below Deckler's Cliff reaching after about 1 mile the
precipitous Gammon Head. Gammon Head looks down on
the two lonely but very tempting beaches in Maceley Cove,
reached by steep path. (A track inland will take you, after
$1\frac{1}{4}$ miles, to East Prawle if in need of refreshment; you can
rejoin the Path by another track to Prawle Point from East
Prawle.)

Follow the indentations of the coast to the Coast
Guard station on Prawle Point.

*In the late summer, on the whole sector from Salcombe, the
National Trust leaflet mentions that many butterflies can be
found in sheltered places: small coppers, pearl bordered
fritillaries and silver studded blue.*

*Prawle Point is an excellent viewing place for migrating
birds, particularly in the autumn, such as warblers, wagtails,
pipits, wheatears, etc; for waders such as turnstones, curlew,
whimbrel, dunlin, oystercatcher, etc; and for sea birds, such as
kittiwakes, shearwaters, terns, etc.*

Once round the Point there is a quite dramatic change of
scene. Stretching in front of you is a 'shelf' of pasture and
growing crops. You get here a fine view of the geologist's
'raised beach'. The 'shelf' was part of the sea bed; the original
line of cliff, of up to 300ft in height, can be seen $\frac{1}{2}$ mile or more
inland, complete with caves (see Geology, Appendix).

The Path from Prawle Point is not too clear but proceeds
in front of the Coast Guard cottages and then along the
seaward edge of the fields, along the edge of the low cliff,
turning slightly inland opposite Ballsaddle Rock. There is
then a track to the small but pleasant Lannacombe Beach of
sands and rocks, with good bathing. The capacity of the very
small car park protects the beach from overcrowding.

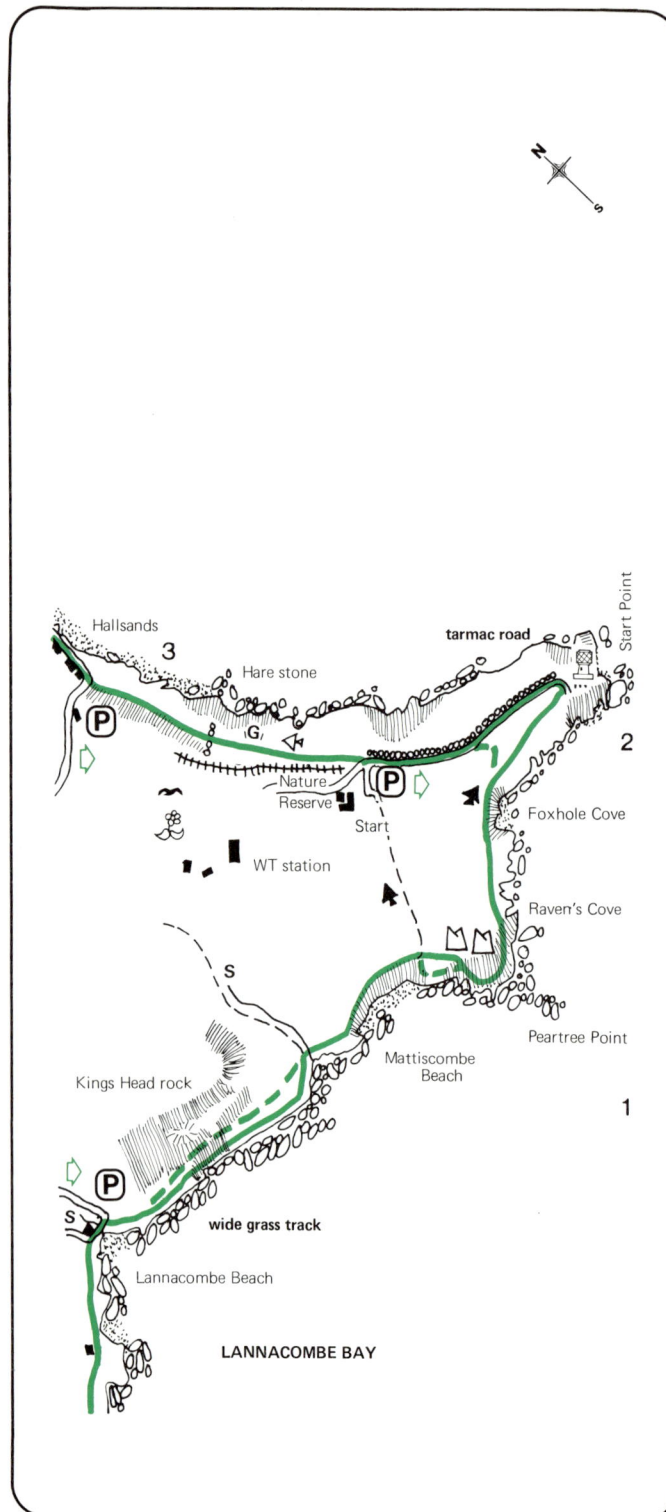

Hallsands

3

Hare stone

tarmac road

Start Point

P

G

2

Nature
Reserve

P

Start

Foxhole Cove

WT station

Raven's Cove

s

Peartree Point

Kings Head rock

Mattiscombe
Beach

1

P

s

wide grass track

Lannacombe Beach

LANNACOMBE BAY

9 Lannacombe Bay-Start Point-Hallsands

3½ miles 5½km   From Plymouth 44¾ miles 72¼km

Going: up to Start Point a pleasant walk with no problems;
not very attractive beyond.

The Path lies up through the bracken from Lannacombe
Beach. From just before the rocky Peartree Point the Path
round Start Point to Hallsands is way-marked by blue paint.
It keeps close to the coastline above the long Mattiscombe
Beach (swimming can be dangerous). Nearing Start Point you
have to climb a bit to the top of the ridge which ends in the
Point; you then come out on the road leading to Start Point
Lighthouse and a fine view of the next 15 miles of coast with
Slapton Ley, the largest stretch of inland fresh water in Devon,
bounded by the 5-mile barrier of shingle and sand, Slapton
Sands.

*Start Point Lighthouse was built in 1836; 'start' meant
'tail' in Anglo-Saxon and the rocky tail of the Point has been the
gravestone of many ships. The Lighthouse may be visited every
afternoon from Monday to Saturday. Start Point is a Nature
Reserve and in the spring and autumn a fine viewing spot for
migrating birds: swallows, wagtails, warblers, wheatears, etc.
Also for sea birds flying west in the autumn: kittiwakes,
gannets, terns, shearwaters, etc.*

The route of the Path follows the lighthouse road inland
for about ½ mile and then at the car-park turns off along the
cliff-top through gorse and bracken. Follow the blue waymark
down into Hallsands.

*At the end of the 19th-century a quantity of shingle was
removed from the beach at Hallsands for construction work in
Plymouth docks. This weakened the sea defences and after a
storm in 1917 the houses on the seaward side of the main street
were undermined and eventually collapsed. There is now only
trace of one building. There are pictures of the tragedy in the
local pubs.*

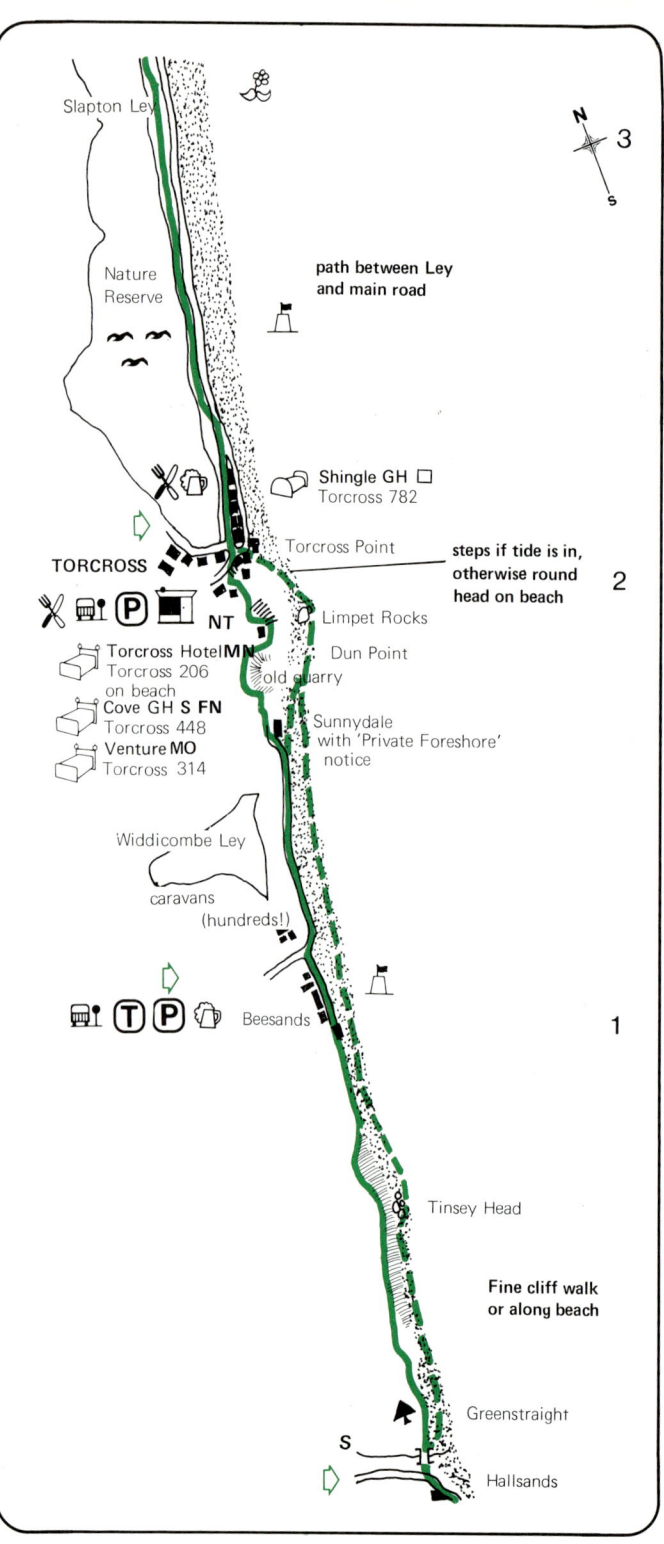

Slapton Ley

Nature
Reserve

**path between Ley
and main road**

Shingle GH ☐
Torcross 782

Torcross Point

**steps if tide is in,
otherwise round
head on beach**

TORCROSS

NT

Limpet Rocks

Torcross Hotel **M N**
Torcross 206
on beach

Dun Point

old quarry

Cove GH **S FN**
Torcross 448

Sunnydale
with 'Private Foreshore'
notice

Venture **M O**
Torcross 314

Widdicombe Ley

caravans

(hundreds!)

Beesands

1

Tinsey Head

**Fine cliff walk
or along beach**

Greenstraight

S

Hallsands

10 Hallsands-Torcross-Slapton Ley

3½ miles 5½km From Plymouth 48¼ miles 77¾km

Going: no difficulty as far as Torcross. Beyond Torcross the 2½ mile straight stretch of Path behind Slapton Sands, and a few feet from the main road as far as Strete Gate, has little to commend it. There is no footpath from Strete Gate for the next 4 miles to the other side of Stoke Fleming (section 12). If you wish to avoid the road-walking involved there is an hourly bus service from Torcross through to Stoke Fleming.

From Hallsands the route of the Path runs along the coast, clear and without difficulty.

Beesands is a small fishing village with a line of cottages overlooking the sea; it was the victim of an air-raid in 1943. There is a good pub, the Cricket, and on the north side of the village a large unattractive caravan site.

Beyond Sunnydale the Path climbs inland for ½ mile to avoid a disused slate quarry before dropping down to Torcross (Tor = rock), formerly a small fishing hamlet (a few old fishermen's cottages still remain) but now catering for the holiday-maker. If the state of the tide allows you can walk along the beach to avoid the climb above Torcross. All facilities provided at Torcross, including an old pub, the Start Bay. The village stands at the south end of Slapton Ley, a large stretch of freshwater noted for its variety of wild life.

Slapton Ley, 2 miles long and covering 250 acres, is an important Nature Reserve. In the nearby village of Slapton is the Slapton Ley Field Study Centre which controls entry to the Reserve. There is also a bird-watching post of the Devon Bird-Watching and Preservation Society. The Ley is a particular centre of attraction in spring and autumn for migrating birds and also for wintering flocks of ducks: mallard, pochard, tufted duck, etc. The attraction in both instances is the abundant supply of water plants in this shallow stretch of water. The marshes of the Higher Ley are a breeding place for reed warblers; sedge warblers are frequent visitors. Roger Burrows, in The Naturalist in Devon and Cornwall, mentions a reed warbler ringed in the Ley in August 1965 which was recovered in Spanish North Africa only 6 weeks later. The Ley abounds in insects, much appreciated by birds arriving in the spring—swallows, martins, warblers, wagtails, etc. The aquatic plants of the Ley are themselves of interest and include some rarities. Of the insects, 17 species of dragon-fly have been recorded.

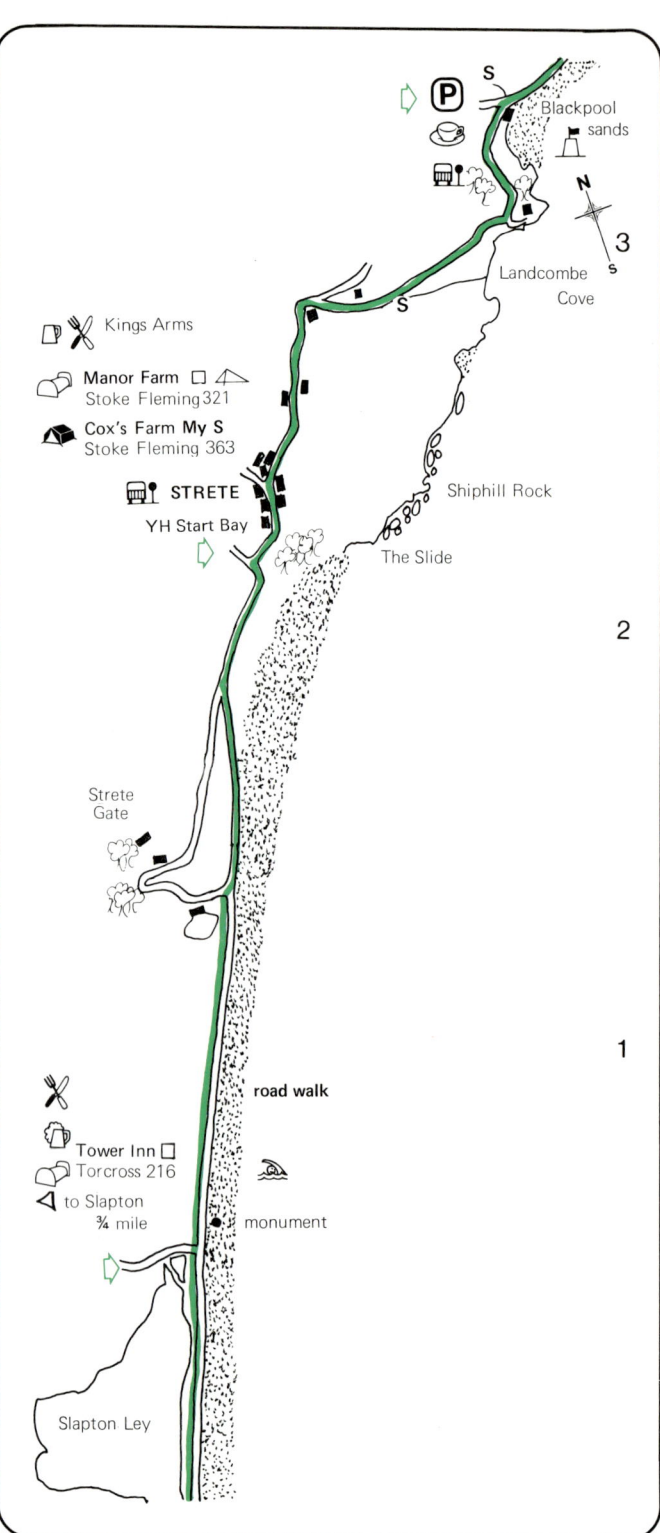

Blackpool sands

Landcombe Cove

N

3

S

Kings Arms

Manor Farm
Stoke Fleming 321

Cox's Farm My S
Stoke Fleming 363

STRETE

YH Start Bay

Shiphill Rock

The Slide

2

Strete Gate

1

road walk

Tower Inn
Torcross 216

to Slapton
¾ mile

monument

Slapton Ley

11 Slapton Ley-Blackpool Sands

$3\frac{1}{2}$ miles $5\frac{1}{2}$km From Plymouth $51\frac{3}{4}$ miles $83\frac{1}{4}$km

Going: as mentioned on the previous section, the Path runs rather boringly in a straight line behind Slapton Beach as far as Strete Gate. Beyond Strete Gate you have to take to the road for 4 miles, but this can be not only uncomfortable but dangerous in the summer season. If you prefer, you can take a bus via Blackpool Sands to Stoke Fleming (section 12) where you can rejoin the footpath. Ask on the bus for Windward Corner.

Slapton Beach was used by the Americans for rehearsals of the Normandy landings, and this is commemorated by a monument half-way along the Beach.

Whether you go on foot or by bus, you can break your journey at the villages of Slapton and Strete. Both are of interest. There is a Youth Hostel and two pubs in Slapton, the Queens Arms and the Tower. In Strete there is the King's Arms.

Blackpool Sands, a delightful spot out of the season. becomes crowded in summer. It was the object of another kind of invasion in 1304 when raiders from Brittany landed there, to be repulsed by the men of Dartmouth.

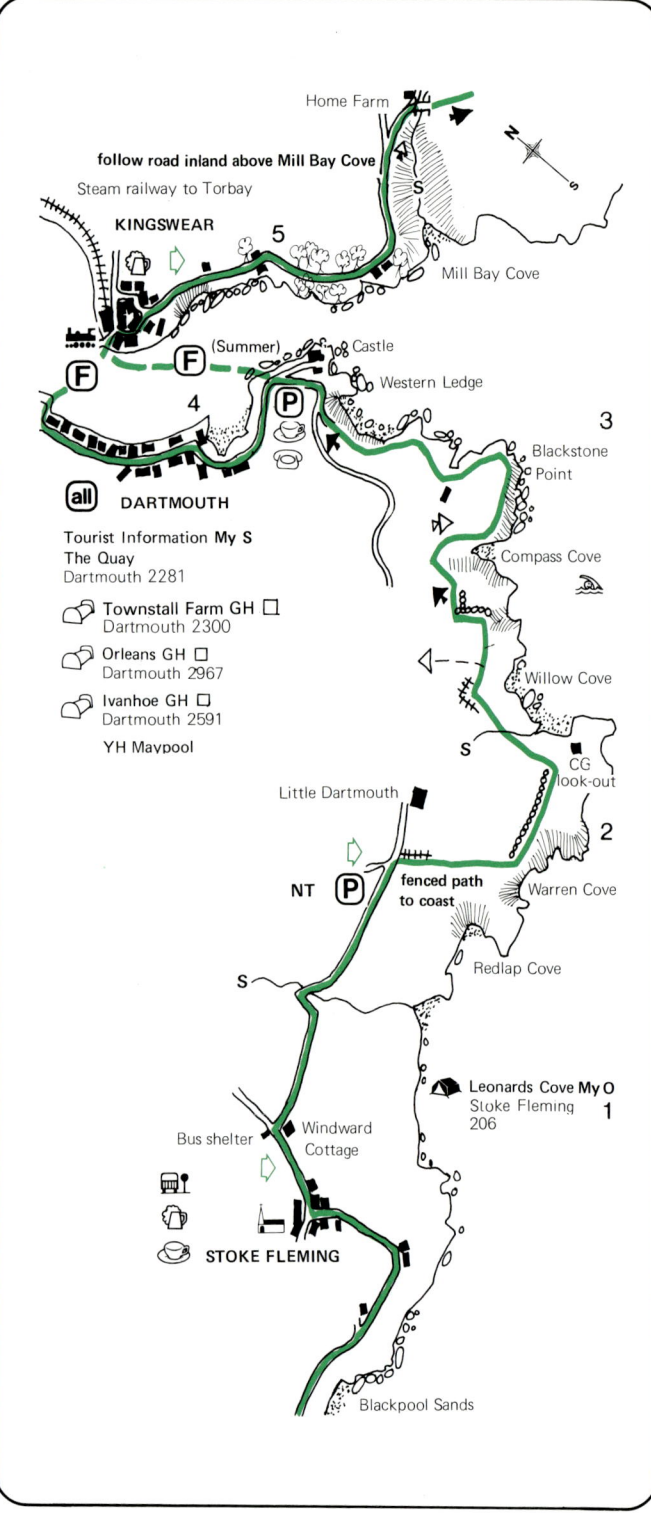

Home Farm

follow road inland above Mill Bay Cove

Steam railway to Torbay

KINGSWEAR 5

Mill Bay Cove

(Summer) Castle

Western Ledge

F F

3

Blackstone Point

4

DARTMOUTH

Compass Cove

Tourist Information My S
The Quay
Dartmouth 2281

Willow Cove

Townstall Farm GH □
Dartmouth 2300

S

Orleans GH □
Dartmouth 2967

CG look-out

Ivanhoe GH □
Dartmouth 2591

2

YH Maypool

Little Dartmouth

Warren Cove

NT P fenced path to coast

Redlap Cove

S

Leonards Cove My O
Stoke Fleming
206 1

Bus shelter Windward Cottage

STOKE FLEMING

Blackpool Sands

12 Blackpool Sands-Dartmouth-Mill Bay Cove

5¾ miles 8¼ km   From Plymouth 57½ miles 91½ km

Going: on the main road as far as Stoke Fleming; from there to
Dartmouth a pleasant coast walk with fine views. Over the
estuary the Path again follows along a road from Kingswear,
but a quiet country one this time. (Kingswear to Exmouth
—Section 18—has a great deal of road walking and the
problem of the seasonal ferry over the Exe. To avoid this you
can take the train all the way.)

The main road (and the bus) takes you to Stoke Fleming
from Blackpool Sands. Stoke Fleming has an impressive
church with some good 14th-century brasses. From the
centre of the village follow the main road northwards for
about ½ mile until, on the left, you come to some playing
fields (Windward Corner). Take the turning on the right
opposite the playing fields. This secondary road twists and
dips through quiet pastureland and brings you, after about
another ¾ mile, to a National Trust Car Park. A signpost
opposite the Car Park directs you to the Coast Path which
takes you towards the coastline before turning east, along the
lofty cliff top covered with gorse and bracken, past a Coast
Guard lookout. The Path then gradually descends, through
thick undergrowth, to Compass Cove—nice little shingle beach
with good swimming—and round Blackstone Point to the road
and Dartmouth Castle, on the outskirts of Dartmouth itself.

*Dartmouth (population 6000), in a beautiful setting on the
steep slopes leading down to the River Dart, has a long history.
By the 12th century it was already a seaport of some importance,
departure point for the Crusades, and throughout the Middle
Ages enjoyed a flourishing trade with the Continent. After a
period of decline the exploitation of the Newfoundland fishing
grounds brought about a revival in the 17th century. Its most
famous institution is the Royal Naval College, prominent on the
hillside above the town, which has numbered many royal
princes among its pupils. Dartmouth Castle was a 15th-century
defence against French raiders; the other small fort farther up
river was built by Henry VIII. The churches of St Petroc (by
Dartmouth Castle) and St Saviour's (in the town) are worth
visiting. There are some fine old houses and old pubs near the
waterfront.*

Lower Ferry runs from Dartmouth to Kingswear daily all
the year round, last departure 22.50. There is also a vehicle
ferry. A ferry runs in the summer from the Castle to Dartmouth.

There is no official Coast Path open yet from Kingswear
round to Man Sands, 2½ miles south of Brixham. At the time
of writing the Countryside Commission are still negotiating
the rights-of-way. As an alternative you can walk to Man
Sands by quiet country road, starting at the street in Kingswear
running parallel to the estuary and up Alma Steps. This comes
out as a country road between hedges high above Mill Bay Cove.

33

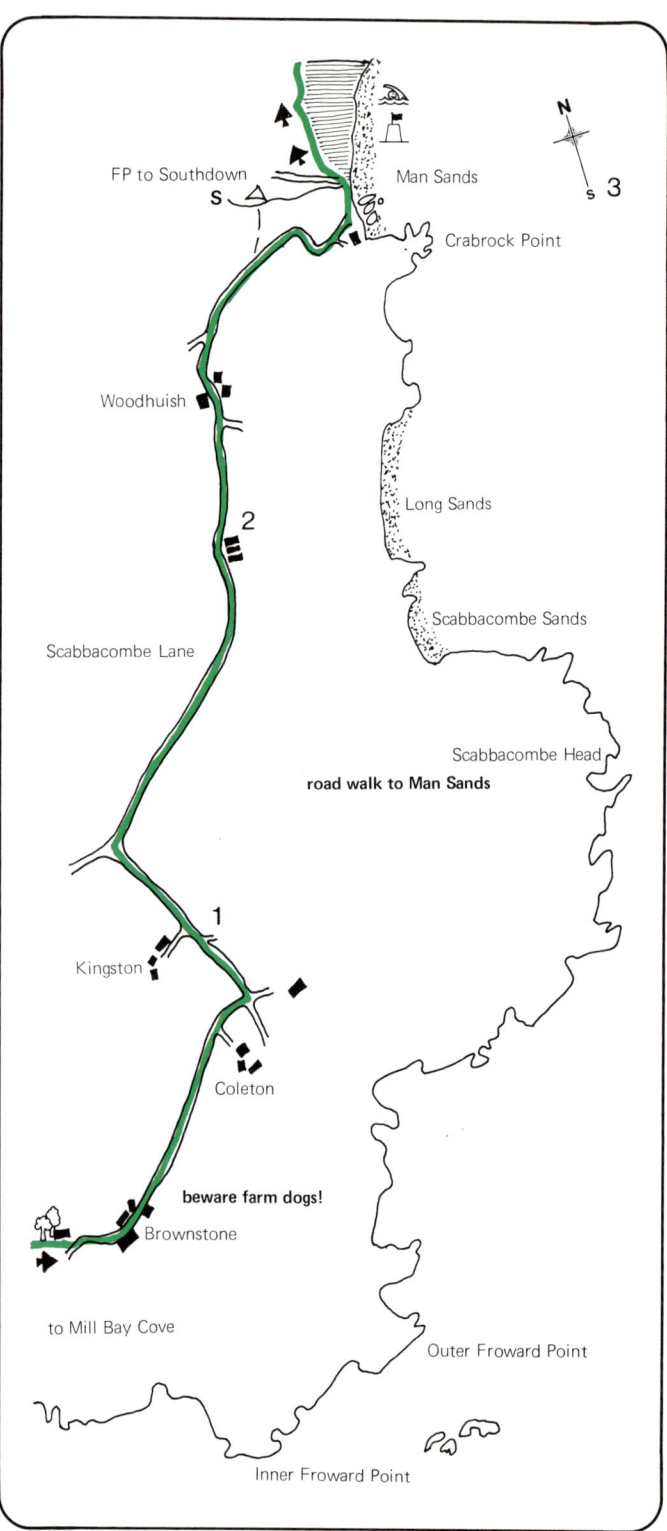

FP to Southdown

Man Sands

Crabrock Point

Woodhuish

Long Sands

2

Scabbacombe Sands

Scabbacombe Lane

Scabbacombe Head

road walk to Man Sands

1

Kingston

Coleton

beware farm dogs!

Brownstone

to Mill Bay Cove

Outer Froward Point

Inner Froward Point

N
S 3

13 Mill Bay Cove-Man Sands

3½ miles 5½km From Plymouth 61 miles 98km

Going: this is all country road, but one on which you are not likely to find much traffic, except perhaps on Bank Holidays.

As the sector from Kingswear to Brixham and Torquay (sections 13 and 14) is mostly by road you may decide to go from Kingswear straight through to Torquay by public transport. In the summer you can get a bus from Kingswear that not only runs to Torquay but to Babbacombe on the north boundary of the resort from where you can rejoin the Path (see section 15). Outside the summer months the bus goes to Paignton Bus Station where you can catch another one to Torquay and Babbacombe. For those interested in steam railways there is the Torbay Steam Railway which runs a service from Kingswear to Paignton in the summer and in the Easter holidays. At Kingswear the station adjoins the Ferry terminal, and in Paignton is only a few yards from the Bus and British Rail Stations. The Torbay Steam Railway is run by a private company which took over the line when British Rail proposed to shut it.

Continue the road you started from Kingswear, taking the right-hand fork to Home Farm just above Mill Bay Cove. Just before the buildings a lane turns sharp right off the road to cross the stream and climb steeply through the small copse. The lane joins a farm-track at a pair of cottages and Brownstone Farm. The way then lies along a country road through undulating pastureland with wide views across the countryside.

The metalled road, usable by cars, becomes a rough track (no cars) leading down to Man Sands. Allow 1½-1¾ hours from Kingswear Ferry.

Apart from one or two former Coast Guard cottages, Man Sands is quite isolated. You can swim from its small pebble beach.

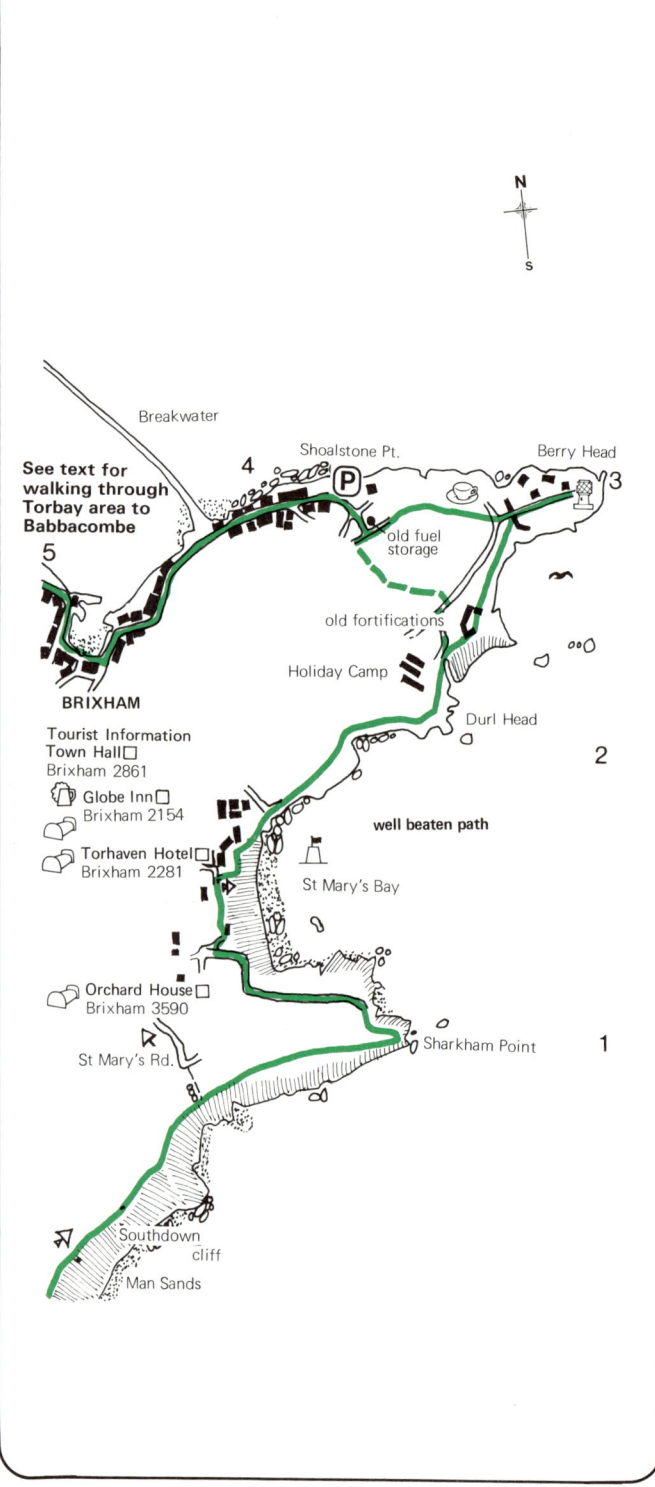

Breakwater

See text for
walking through
Torbay area to
Babbacombe

Shoalstone Pt.

Berry Head

4

P

old fuel
storage

3

5

old fortifications

BRIXHAM

Holiday Camp

Tourist Information
Town Hall □
Brixham 2861

Durl Head

2

Globe Inn □
Brixham 2154

Torhaven Hotel □
Brixham 2281

well beaten path

St Mary's Bay

Orchard House □
Brixham 3590

St Mary's Rd.

Sharkham Point

1

Southdown
cliff

Man Sands

14 Man Sands-Brixham

5 miles 8km   From Plymouth 66 miles 106km

Going: this section takes you right through to the other (west) side of Brixham. Pleasant enough cliff walking until Brixham is reached; you are then conscious the whole time of the looming built-up area.

A very steep climb from Man Sands to the top of the 420ft Southdown Cliff is followed by a good walk over springy turf dotted with gorse bushes with one or two easy slopes. You come to Sharkham Point, with fine views but utterly spoiled by old cars and other rubbish dumped there. There are traces of former mining activity on the Point.

From Sharkham Point the Path curls round St Mary's Bay as it descends.

St Mary's Bay has a good beach of pebble and sand.

As it climbs out of the Bay through thick undergrowth, the Path hugs the cliff-edge round Durl Head, an impressive crag with folded limestone strata. You then come to Berry Head Common—you will notice a large air navigation beacon—and on the tip of the Head, the Lighthouse.

The whole of Berry Head has been declared a Country Park. In spring and early summer the cliffs are the breeding place of fulmars, kittiwakes, guillemots, and razorbills, as well as the herring gull. There are traces on the Head of an Iron-Age cliff fort; the other massive remains are of fortifications built in 1803 at a time when invasion by Napoleon was feared.

The Path is easily followed into Brixham.

Brixham, now a sprawling resort, has been an important fishing port for centuries. The harbour still preserves much of its character. William of Orange landed in Brixham in 1688 to become William III, commemorated by a statue. As you come off Berry Head you pass Berry Head House (now a hotel) where the Reverend Lyte, writer of 'Abide with me' lived. The large brick gasometer-looking enclosure near the Hotel was built in the 1939-45 war as a fuel dump.

If you are not anxious to stop in Brixham or walk its pavements you can catch a 117 bus from Berry Head Road, leading from the base of Berry Head right to Fishcombe Road where you can join the Path again on the other side of the town.

The Path from here to Oddicombe Beach on the other side of Torquay is mainly town walking. An excellent book on walks in the Torbay area, including the Coastal Path is published by Torbay Public Works Department, price 20p.

For our notes on walking through the Torbay area—Brixham, Paignton, and Torquay—see Appendix.

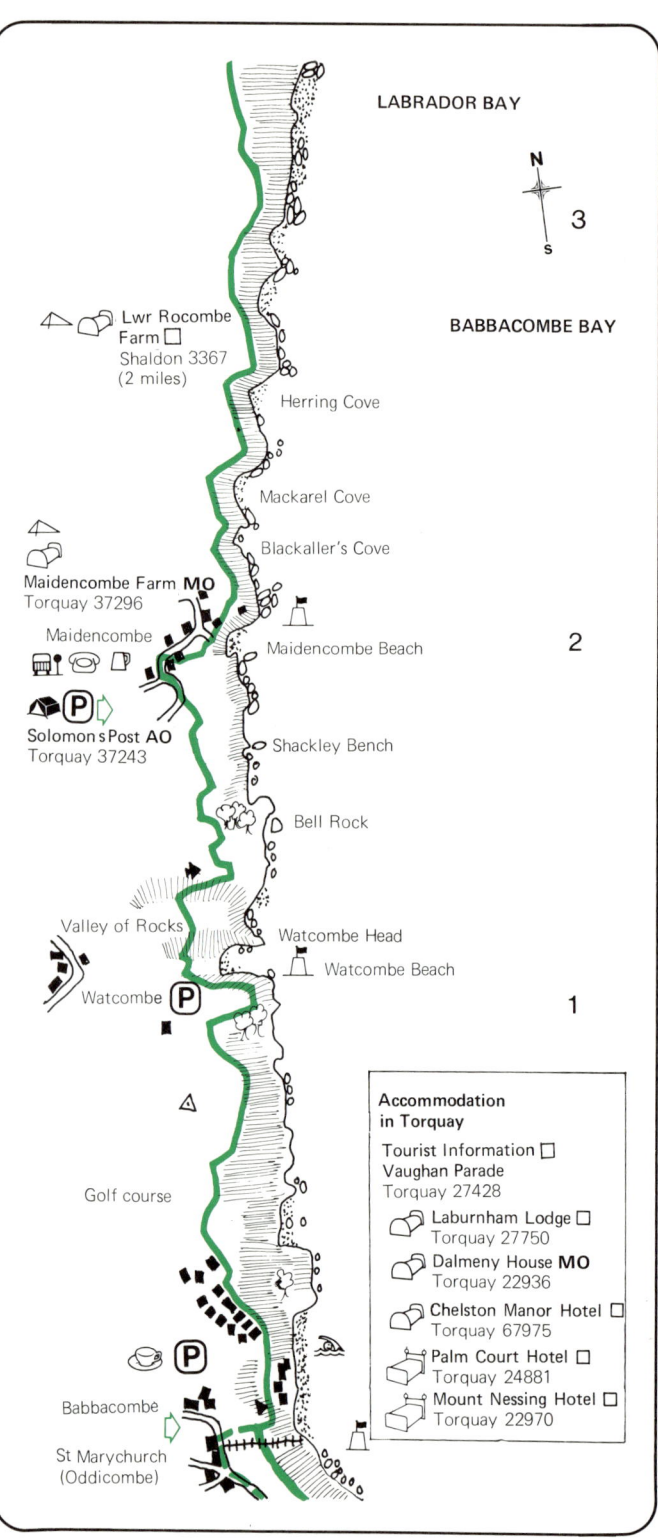

LABRADOR BAY

BABBACOMBE BAY

Lwr Rocombe
Farm
Shaldon 3367
(2 miles)

Herring Cove

Mackarel Cove

Blackaller's Cove

Maidencombe Farm **MO**
Torquay 37296

Maidencombe

Maidencombe Beach

Solomons Post **AO**
Torquay 37243

Shackley Bench

Bell Rock

Valley of Rocks

Watcombe Head

Watcombe Beach

Watcombe

Golf course

Babbacombe

St Marychurch
(Oddicombe)

**Accommodation
in Torquay**

Tourist Information
Vaughan Parade
Torquay 27428

Laburnham Lodge
Torquay 27750

Dalmeny House **MO**
Torquay 22936

Chelston Manor Hotel
Torquay 67975

Palm Court Hotel
Torquay 24881

Mount Nessing Hotel
Torquay 22970

3

2

1

15 Oddicombe (Torquay)-Labrador Bay

*6¾ miles 11km   From Plymouth 76¾ miles 123½km

Going: a pleasant seaside promenade at first, undulating through woods from Oddicombe Beach; touching three more beaches en route. Beyond Maidencombe you have a country path rising and falling quite steeply as it crosses two or three combes.

The Coast Path leaves Oddicombe Beach near the lower station of the Cliff Railway and then starts climbing. Passing above Petit Tor beach it enters a patch of thick woodland, emerging at Watcombe Beach in a completely wooded setting. A steep climb out of Watcombe, helped by some steps (with fine glimpses of the sea from the cliff top, through the trees), brings you eventually to the delightful village of Maidencombe.

Maidencombe has a sandy beach, quite a sun trap. There is the Thatched House pub (open in the season) among the other thatched cottages of the village which seems quite unspoiled—although, because of the beach, there may be a lot of visitors in July and August.

From Maidencombe the route is along a field path close to the cliff edge which is out of sight for most of the way because of the thick hedge, undergrowth, and trees bordering the Path on the seaward side. For the 1½ miles from Maidencombe to where the Path comes out on the road (next section) you pass through fields and woods, dipping and rising, with the combes running down to the sea, and without a human habitation in sight—ideal for country picnics.

* From Meadfoot Beach (Torquay) see Appendix.

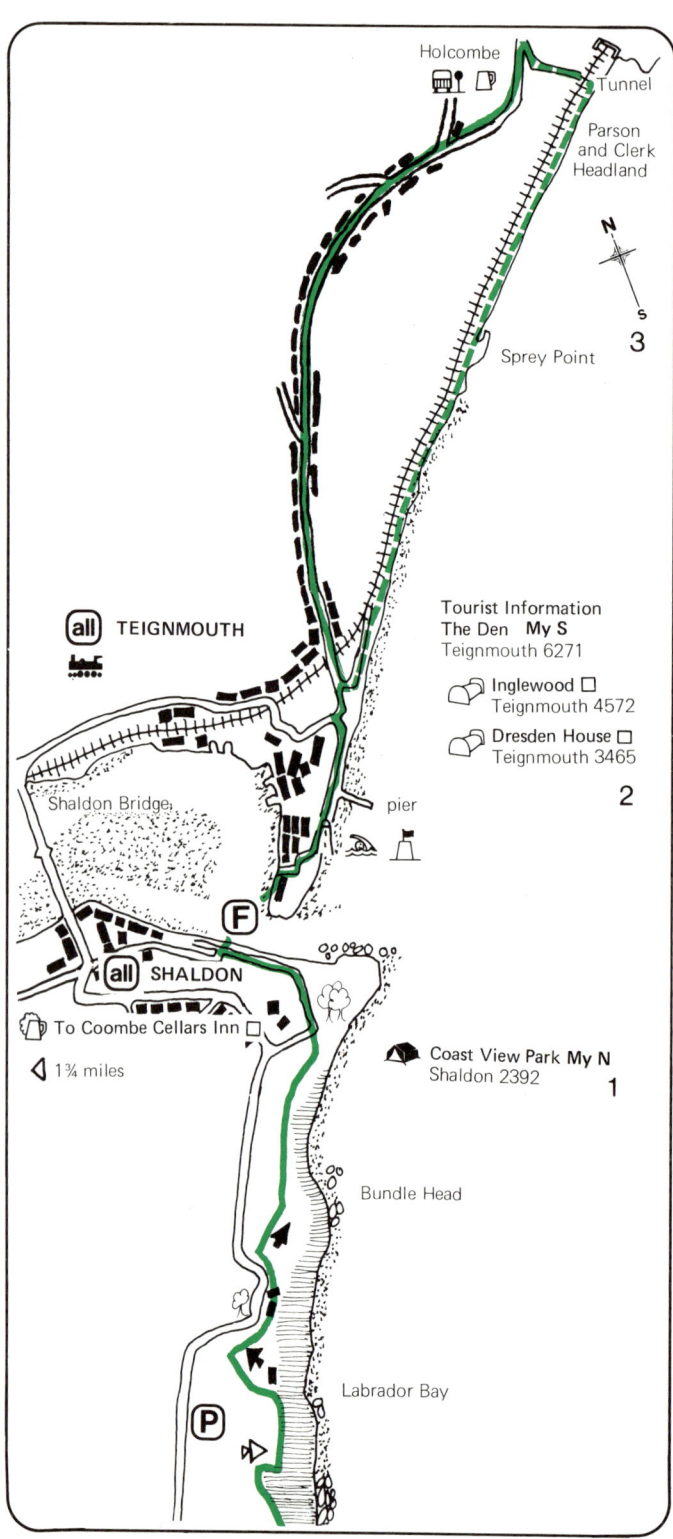

Holcombe

Tunnel

Parson
and Clerk
Headland

N

S

3

Sprey Point

all TEIGNMOUTH

Tourist Information
The Den **My S**
Teignmouth 6271

Inglewood ☐
Teignmouth 4572

Dresden House ☐
Teignmouth 3465

2

Shaldon Bridge

pier

F

all SHALDON

To Coombe Cellars Inn ☐

◁ 1¾ miles

Coast View Park **My N**
Shaldon 2392

1

Bundle Head

P

Labrador Bay

16 Labrador-Teignmouth-Holcombe

4 miles 6½km   From Plymouth 80¾ miles 130km

Going: a steep climb out of Labrador Bay then down to
Shaldon and across the river Teign. From Teignmouth a cliff
walk or along the 'promenade' by the Side of the railway
and a few feet above the sands.

Leaving Labrador Bay, and to avoid a private estate, the
Path is diverted inland up a steep slope to the main A379 road
for about ¼ mile. On busy days this stretch is extremely
dangerous: take great care. On the main road you come to a
stile and signpost indicating where the Coast Path continues
across fields which slope gradually down to Shaldon, giving
you a fine view over Teignmouth and the coast beyond. The
red Permian sandstone which colours the Devon coastal
landscape shows up prominently.

Although there is a bridge over the River Teign ½ mile up
river between Shaldon and Teignmouth, there is a frequent
all-the-year-round ferry service near the mouth of the river
which walkers will find convenient. The ferry leaves Shaldon
by the foreshore (Marine Parade); last departure in July and
August 22.00. Other times 17.00, an hour or two later in early
summer.

*Teignmouth (population 12,000) can probably boast the
earliest documentary historical record of all coastal towns of the
south-west as its seal dates back to the reign of Ethelred the
Unready (1002), and it is mentioned in a charter of Edward the
Confessor in 1044. A port of some importance for nearly 1000
years, it is one of the first resorts to be developed in Devon.
Keats and Fanny Burney stayed there early in the last century.
The port is still active mainly with the export of potter's clay
which is brought from farther up the river. Granite from
Dartmoor was shipped from here in 1820 for the building of
London Bridge—the one which has ended up being re-erected
in the USA. Teignmouth suffered from raids by the French in
the 14th and 17th centuries. In the Second World War it was the
target of many hit-and-run air raids. It has a fine sandy beach.*

There is a sea promenade running along the railway north
of Teignmouth; you can use this or the official Path which runs
inland along the cliff to the road near Holcombe. You can also,
if tide permits, walk along the sands. Walkers on the
promenade take the short lane (Smugglers' Lane) inland to
Holcombe, where the railway enters a tunnel. The rock pillar is
The Parson and the Clerk. The bus (½ hourly) will take you, if
you wish, straight through Dawlish (ask for the Catholic
Church). There are two pubs in Holcombe.

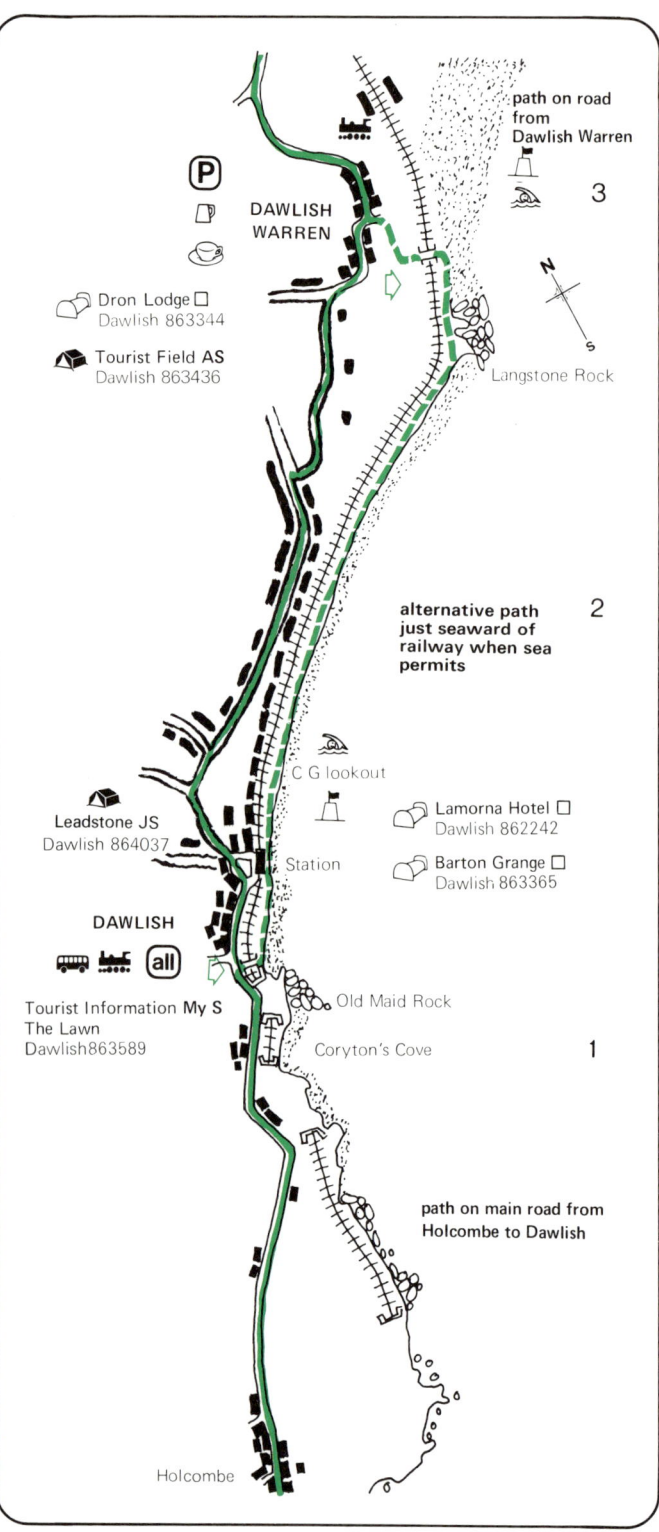

path on road
from
Dawlish Warren

3

DAWLISH
WARREN

Dron Lodge □
Dawlish 863344

Tourist Field AS
Dawlish 863436

Langstone Rock

N

S

alternative path
just seaward of
railway when sea
permits

2

C G lookout

Lamorna Hotel □
Dawlish 862242

Leadstone JS
Dawlish 864037

Barton Grange □
Dawlish 863365

Station

DAWLISH

all

Tourist Information My S
The Lawn
Dawlish863589

Old Maid Rock

Coryton's Cove

1

path on main road from
Holcombe to Dawlish

Holcombe

17 Holcombe-Dawlish-Dawlish Warren

$3\frac{1}{2}$ miles $5\frac{1}{2}$km   From Plymouth $84\frac{1}{4}$ miles $135\frac{1}{2}$km

Going: through Dawlish and then over the low cliff, or along a seaside promenade, or over the sands.

Dawlish is purely what used to be called a small watering-place. Its name is of Saxon origin and there are a few former fishermen's cottages remaining near the Coast Guard lookout. There is a new estate to the north of the town but in the town itself the impression is of Victorian villas.

The official Path starts where the main road turns inland and follows the low cliff line. Alternatively, and if the tide permits, you can follow the promenade alongside the railway. To reach this, there is a footbridge over the railway just down the road from the Catholic church (see section 16). You can also walk along the sands. Of course if you walk through Dawlish you can get down to the sands and the promenade near the square in the centre of the town.

As you turn the corner by Langstone Rock, a huge lump of red sandstone, you can see clearly that the railway has been able to take advantage of a 'raised beach' formation (see Geology Appendix) which provides a 'shelf' on which they have been able to lay the metals all the way from Teignmouth. The need to provide protection both from cliff-falls and from sea-erosion makes this stretch of line very expensive to maintain.

Once round Langstone Rock you come to Dawlish Warren railway station and, stretching out into the estuary of the river Exe, Dawlish Warren.

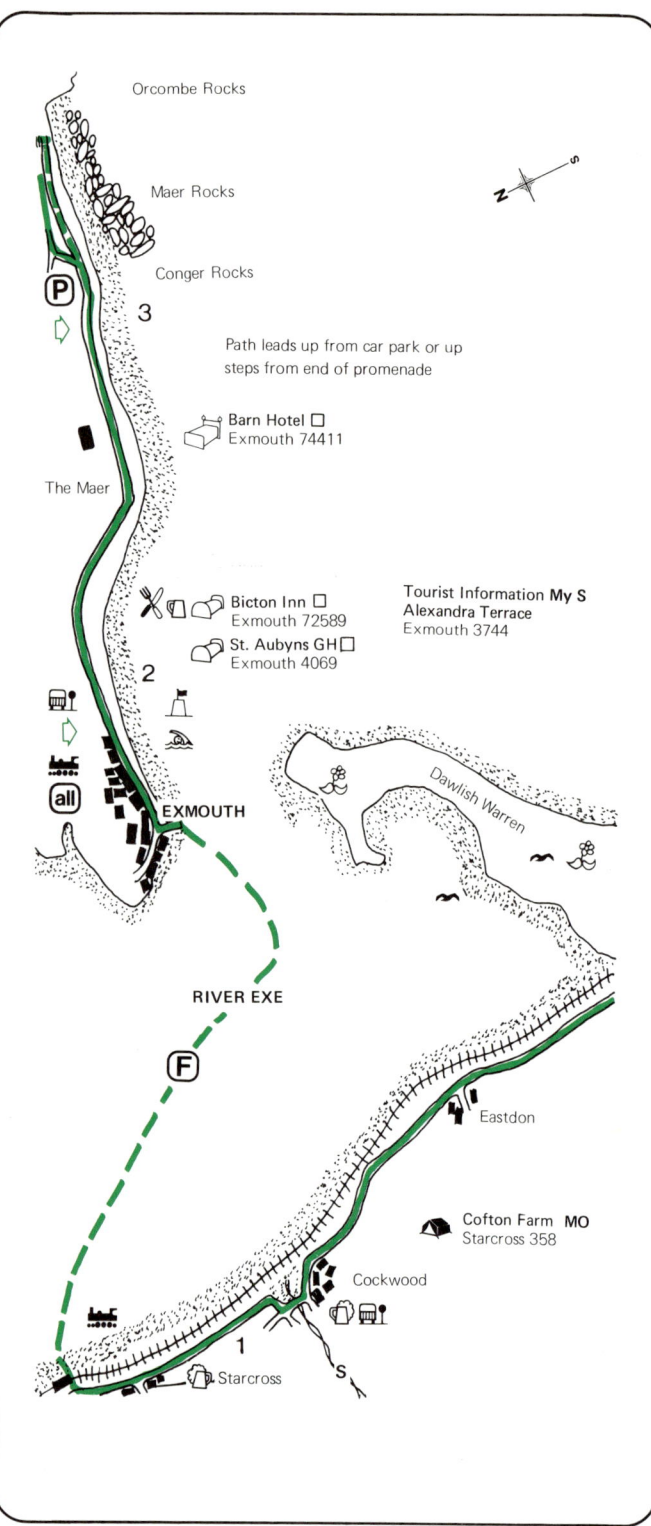

Orcombe Rocks

Maer Rocks

Conger Rocks

P 3

Path leads up from car park or up
steps from end of promenade

🛏 Barn Hotel □
Exmouth 74411

The Maer

✕🍴 ⬦ 🛏 Bicton Inn □
Exmouth 72589
🛏 St. Aubyns GH □
Exmouth 4069

Tourist Information **My S**
Alexandra Terrace
Exmouth 3744

2

🚂

all

EXMOUTH

Dawlish Warren

RIVER EXE

F

Eastdon

⛺ Cofton Farm **MO**
Starcross 358

Cockwood

🍺🛝 1

🚂

🛏 Starcross S

18 Dawlish Warren-Starcross-Exmouth

$3\frac{1}{2}$ miles (not including ferry) $5\frac{1}{2}$ km   From Plymouth $87\frac{3}{4}$ miles 141km

Going: to get from Dawlish Warren across the Exe can only be described as a chore. You have to walk along the road to Starcross, and the ferry from Starcross to Exmouth only runs from the end of May to the end of September (see below).

At first sight Dawlish Warren appears to be nothing but a large unsightly caravan site (with all modern conveniences including a betting shop!). The caravans, however, only cover a small corner of the Warren which extends for $1\frac{1}{2}$ miles, and also encloses a golf course. It is a huge sand spit which is becoming increasingly eroded—in 200 years its width has been halved. It is of great interest to the naturalist both for its salt-water flora and birds; it is a Nature Reserve. The Warren and the Exe estuary provide fine observation posts for migrating waders in the autumn.

To catch the ferry across the Exe you have to get to Starcross. There is no footpath so you have to walk along the road which has nothing to commend it except that it passes Cockwood (pronounced: Co'wood) which has an old pub, the Anchor, to look after your needs.

The Starcross-Exmouth Ferry runs from early May-end September on weekdays; from the end of May-early September on Sundays. Phone Exmouth 72009 for exact dates and timings. If you are unlucky you will have to make a detour of 20 miles inland to Exeter and out again to Exmouth. The bus service (from Cockwood or Starcross) is quite frequent. Alternatively you can catch a train from Dawlish Warren to to Exeter and from Exeter to Exmouth, but the service is infrequent. Whichever way you choose, you should allow at least $1\frac{1}{2}$ hours for the detour.

Starcross, the village terminal of the ferry, has a surprising claim to fame. Its sailing club is the oldest in Britain, perhaps in the world, having been formed in the 18th century. There are four pubs in this small village, the Galleon going back to the 15th century. Another is called the Atmospheric. This refers to the Atmospheric Railway which was one of the less successful undertakings of the famous engineer I K Brunel (1806-59) who had proposed that the system should be used from Exeter to Plymouth. The waggons were propelled by a piston running in a continuous vacuum pipe between the rails. It was a disastrous failure, proving quite impracticable. The red sandstone warehouse in Starcross was one of the pumping stations for the line.

Exmouth (population 26,000) has been a favourite resort since the early 18th century when families from Exeter discovered the attractions of its long sandy beach. Beacon Hill, a street of Georgian houses, contained the residences of Lady Nelson and Lady Byron.

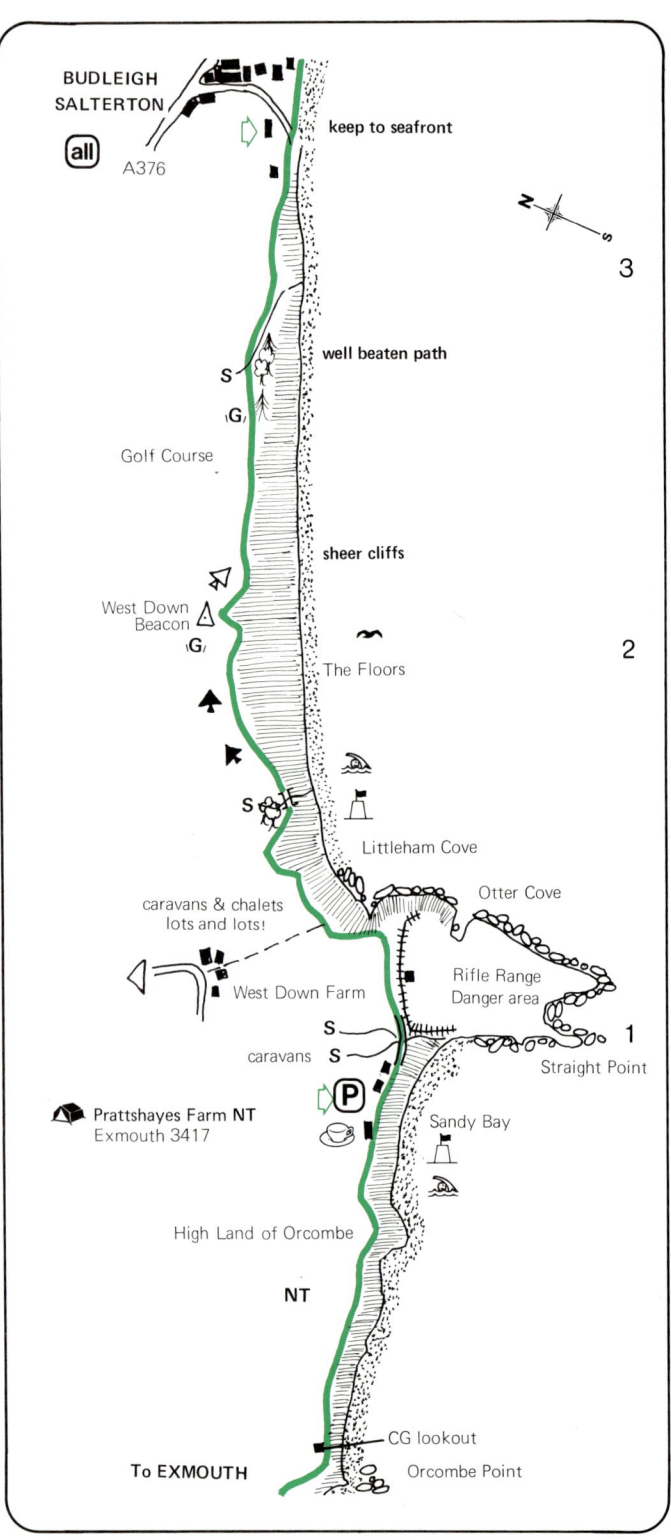

BUDLEIGH
SALTERTON

all

A376

keep to seafront

N

3

well beaten path

S

G

Golf Course

sheer cliffs

West Down
Beacon

G

The Floors

2

S

Littleham Cove

Otter Cove

caravans & chalets
lots and lots!

West Down Farm

Rifle Range
Danger area

S

S

Straight Point

1

caravans

P

Prattshayes Farm NT
Exmouth 3417

Sandy Bay

High Land of Orcombe

NT

CG lookout

To EXMOUTH

Orcombe Point

19 Exmouth-Budleigh Salterton

3½ miles 5½km   From Plymouth 91¼ miles 146½km

Going: after a stroll along the promenade at Exmouth, good high cliff walking all the way to Budleigh Salterton, the scene spoiled only by the large caravan site at Sandy Bay. From Exmouth eastwards for more than 100 miles to the end at Poole Harbour (except the town areas) the Coast Path runs again through what are officially termed 'areas of outstanding natural beauty'.

Once past the large car-park near the end of the Promenade in Exmouth you will see steps and a signpost indicating the Path to Budleigh Salterton, which runs at first between the cliff edge and houses. (The Promenade continues beyond the car-park, coming to an end at Orcombe Rocks. As there is a footpath leading up to the Coast Path from Orcombe Rocks, you can also walk right to the end of the Promenade or along the beach).

The Path soon takes you to the top of the 250ft red sandstone cliff High Land of Orcombe owned by the National Trust. The route of the Path is clear and straightforward but as you start the descent to Sandy Bay the large holiday park intrudes; the Straight Point headland is occupied by a firing-range so you have to walk through the Holiday Park. At the top of the rise you hug the wire fence of the range and then continue through the last of the caravans, keeping to the cliff edge above Littleham Cove.

There is a path down to the beach of shingle and sand much patronised by the Holiday Park occupants.

From the cliff above Littleham Cove you can see the route of the Path making its way gradually up to West Down Beacon, over 400ft high with splendid views.

Between the cliff and the sea is a wild stretch of undercliff called The Floors, covered with thick undergrowth of gorse, bramble, and bushes. You come across a number of such areas on the south Devon-Dorset coast, and they are a favourite haunt of birds, both resident and migrant. Look out for whitethroats, willow warblers, stonechats, goldfinches, and yellowhammers. Kestrels and perhaps a buzzard may show themselves. On the downland, fringing the Path on the other side, you have skylark, wheatear, and corn bunting.

Coming down from West Down Beacon you may be able to see as far as Portland Bill, near Weymouth. The Path runs through some pinewoods and gorse along the boundary of the West Down Golf Course. Keep to the track nearest to the sea and it will bring you to the front at Budleigh Salterton.

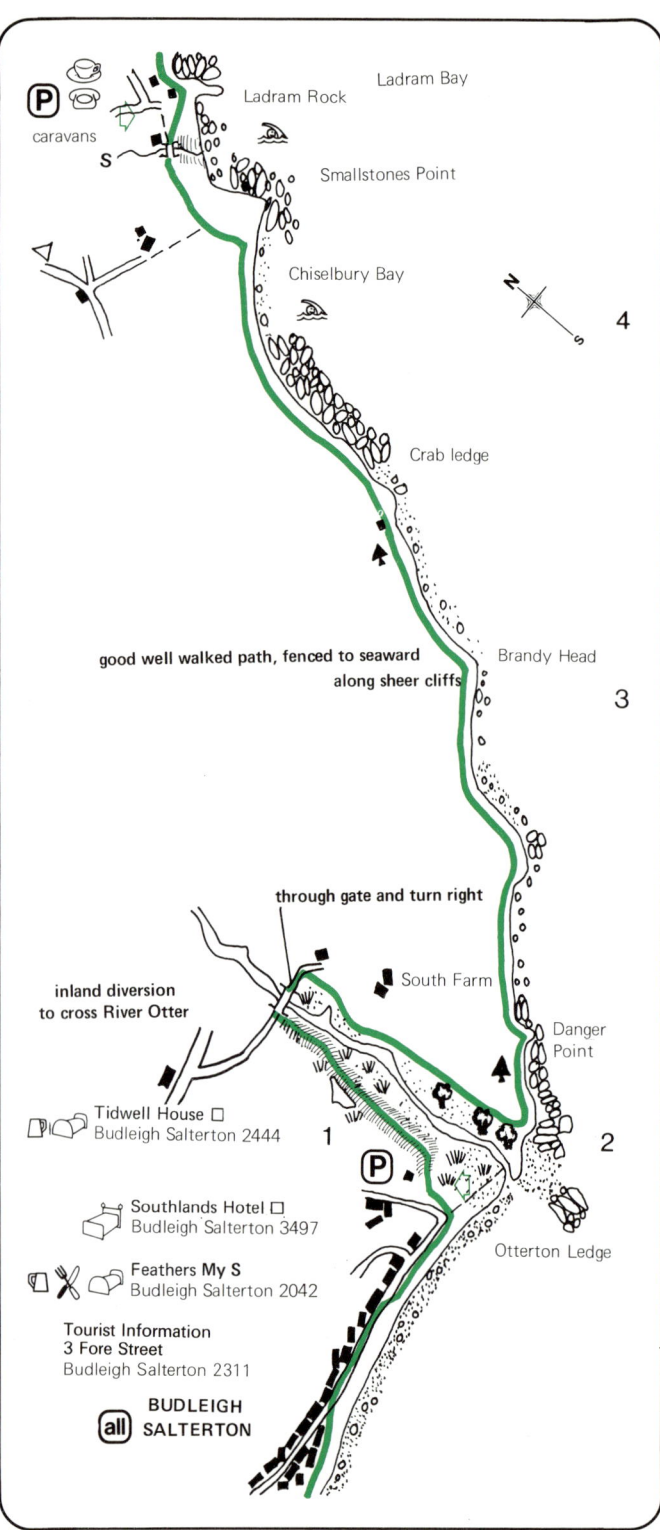

caravans

Ladram Bay

Ladram Rock

Smallstones Point

Chiselbury Bay

Crab ledge

good well walked path, fenced to seaward
along sheer cliffs

Brandy Head

through gate and turn right

South Farm

inland diversion
to cross River Otter

Danger
Point

Tidwell House □
Budleigh Salterton 2444

Southlands Hotel □
Budleigh Salterton 3497

Feathers My S
Budleigh Salterton 2042

Otterton Ledge

Tourist Information
3 Fore Street
Budleigh Salterton 2311

BUDLEIGH
SALTERTON

1

2

3

4

20 Budleigh Salterton-Ladram Bay

4¾ miles 7¾km From Plymouth 96 miles 154¼km

Going: a detour inland, not too long, to cross the river Otter then straightforward cliff walking.

Budleigh Salterton, a small resort whose origins go back to the 13th century or earlier when the salt pans at the mouth of the Otter were worked. The beach of pebbles is steeply shelving, and is a favourite one for the collector of coloured pebbles. The Victorian painter, Sir John Millais, painted his famous picture, The Boyhood of Raleigh *here with part of the sea wall as the setting. 1½ miles inland is the charming village of East Budleigh, a wool port until the 15th century when the Otter began to silt up. Hays Barton, a Tudor farmhouse 1 mile west, was the birthplace of Sir Walter Raleigh in 1552.*

There is no bridge at the mouth of the Otter. Therefore, at the end of the promenade, take the footpath which you will see leads inland on the top of an embankment, near the playing field. This will bring you to a bridge over the river. Cross the bridge and the cattle-grid on the drive up to South Farm. Immediately over the cattle-grid you will see a Coast Path sign directing you seaward along the edge of a wood (not down by the river). At low tide you may be able to wade the Otter at its mouth but take care!

On reaching the cliff the Path turns north-east and continues close to the cliff edge for 2½ miles through pleasant pasture and arable land until, in a wooded coombe running down to the sea, you come to the Ladram Bay Holiday Camp.

On Ladram Bay beach are two famous red sandstone pillars. Refreshments and meals are available.

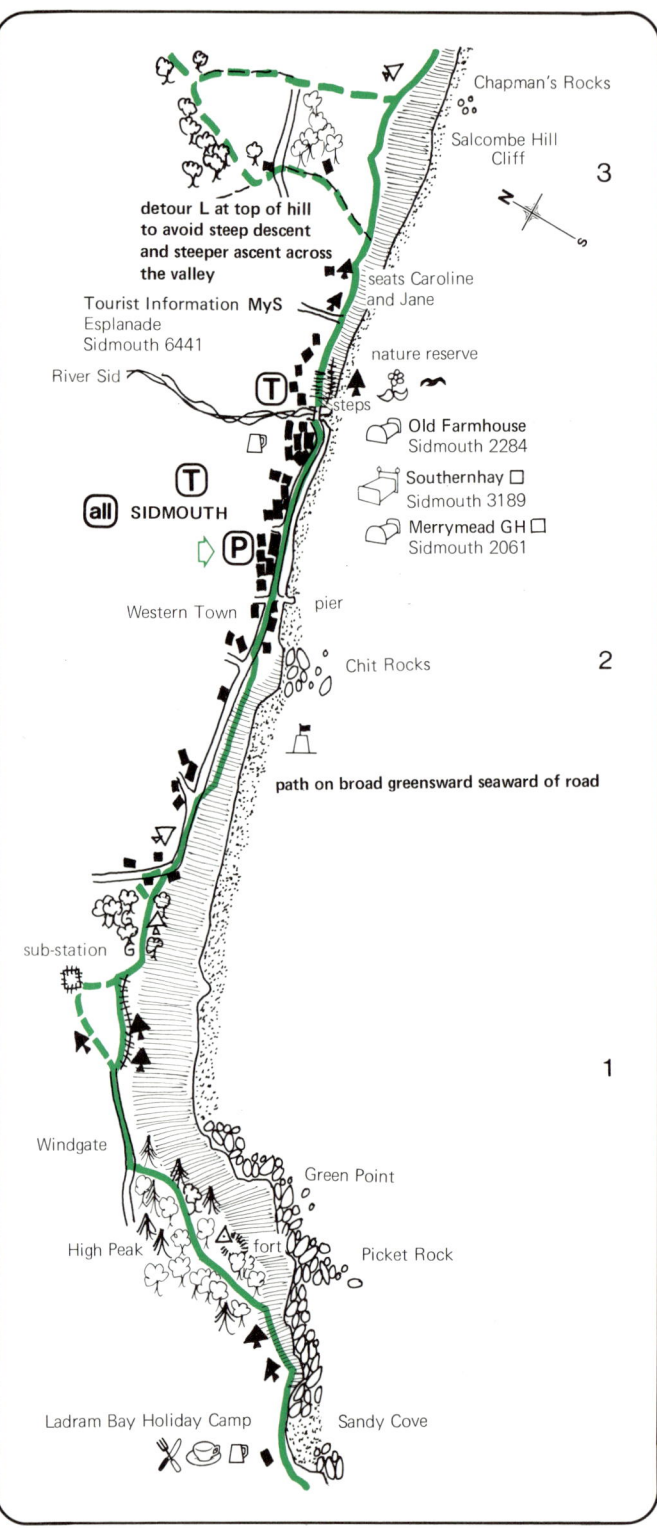

Chapman's Rocks

Salcombe Hill Cliff

3

detour L at top of hill
to avoid steep descent
and steeper ascent across
the valley

seats Caroline
and Jane

Tourist Information MyS
Esplanade
Sidmouth 6441

nature reserve

River Sid

T

steps

Old Farmhouse
Sidmouth 2284

Southernhay □
Sidmouth 3189

T

all SIDMOUTH

Merrymead GH □
Sidmouth 2061

P

Western Town

pier

Chit Rocks

2

path on broad greensward seaward of road

sub-station

1

Windgate

Green Point

High Peak

fort

Picket Rock

Ladram Bay Holiday Camp

Sandy Cove

21 Ladram Bay-Sidmouth-Salcombe Hill Cliff

3½ miles 5½km From Plymouth 99½ miles 160km

Going: two stiff climbs each side of the attractive resort of Sidmouth.

A Coast Path sign by the blue-and-white thatched cottage above the beach at Ladram directs you across fields, past a pub, the Three Rocks (open in summer), up the long climb to the upper slopes of High Peak of over 500ft. The last bit is pretty steep. The slopes are covered by a Forestry Commission conifer plantation. There is no need to climb to the top of High Peak (it is covered in brambles); follow the wide fire-break that runs round the crest. A clear Path leads down on the other side and then climbs up a gorse-covered slope. At the top of the slope is an electric sub-station and, just beyond, a kissing-gate. Beyond this gate, the Path descends through trees to the road running steeply into Sidmouth. There is a wide grass sward on which you can walk almost the whole way down to the Front.

Sidmouth (population 12,000) has been a favourite resort of many since the early 19th century. The little Princess (later Queen) Victoria spent the winter here with her parents in 1819, and many of the Georgian houses of that time still survive. Excellent sandy beach. Good pubs, among others: Marine, Royal London, Balfour Arms.

Cross the footbridge over the River Sid. There are steps and a Coast Path sign showing the way up Salcombe Hill Cliff. The Path forks at a memorial when you reach the top of the hill; take the fork on the seaward side. A left detour avoids the very steep ascent of Higher Dunscombe cliff.

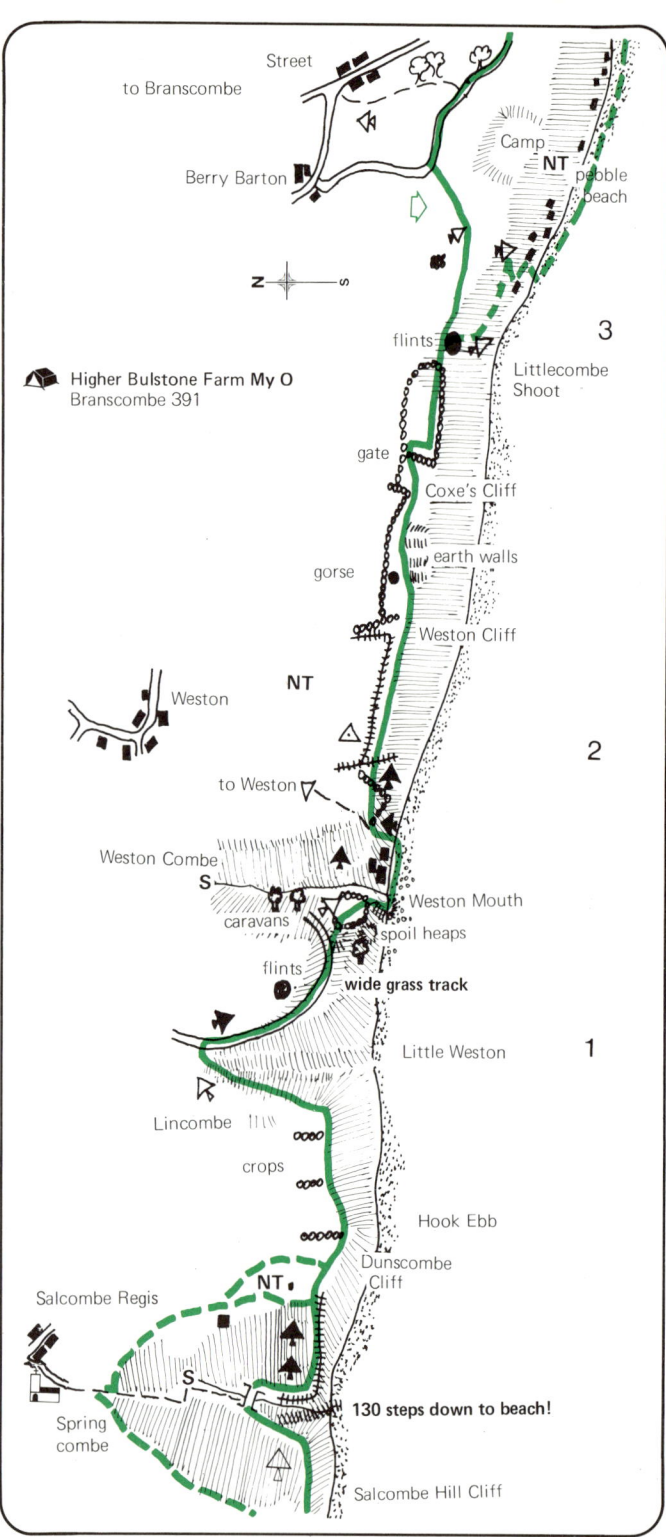

to Branscombe

Street

Berry Barton

Camp

NT pebble beach

N

Higher Bulstone Farm My O
Branscombe 391

flints

3

Littlecombe Shoot

gate

Coxe's Cliff

gorse

earth walls

Weston Cliff

Weston

NT

to Weston

Weston Combe

S

caravans

Weston Mouth

spoil heaps

flints

wide grass track

Little Weston

1

Lincombe

crops

Hook Ebb

Dunscombe Cliff

Salcombe Regis

NT

Spring combe

S

130 steps down to beach!

Salcombe Hill Cliff

52

22 Salcombe Hill Cliff-Branscombe Beach

$3\frac{1}{2}$ miles $5\frac{1}{2}$ km From Plymouth 103 miles $165\frac{1}{2}$ km
Going: two really stiff climbs in this fine unspoiled stretch of coastline.

As you come over Salcombe Hill Cliff (section 21) and begin the descent on the other side, the wide combe running down to Salcombe Mouth, with its two farmsteads and wide fields backed by woodland, makes a wonderful view. The Path runs steeply down to where the stream has cut a gully to the beach. There are 130 steps leading down to Salcombe Beach if you have the energy; you have to climb up them again! You are hardly likely to find anyone else there.

It will be noticed that the formation of the cliffs has changed. The red sandstone has given way to greensand and clays.

From above the beach, the line of the Path runs clearly, climbing the slope of the 500ft Dunscombe Cliff, the boundary of the National Trust's Weston Estate which, with the cliff and village properties farther along at Branscombe, take up most of the coastline between Sidmouth and Branscombe.

From the top of Dunscombe Cliff the Path turns slightly inland to negotiate a steep combe and then drops, through woods, to Weston Mouth, another solitary pebbly beach. There is a steep pull out of Weston Mouth across a rough field, and then along the top of Weston Cliff. The Path, on approaching Coxe's Cliff, turns slightly inland again, runs diagonally across fields and comes out eventually on a farm track.

On the cliff-edge just here, there are traces of an Iron Age or Roman encampment.

Follow the farm track which soon enters wooded slopes on the left. On the right the ground is dotted with mounds which cover waste flints from former lime-workings. You will eventually emerge at the beach at Branscombe Mouth. An interesting alternative path zig-zags down the cliff-face to the beach, and returns.

As you make your way through the woodland, you should be able to glimpse Branscombe church down on your left at the bottom of the slope. It is well worth a visit (see next section) ; there is a footpath running down, over a field, to the churchyard.

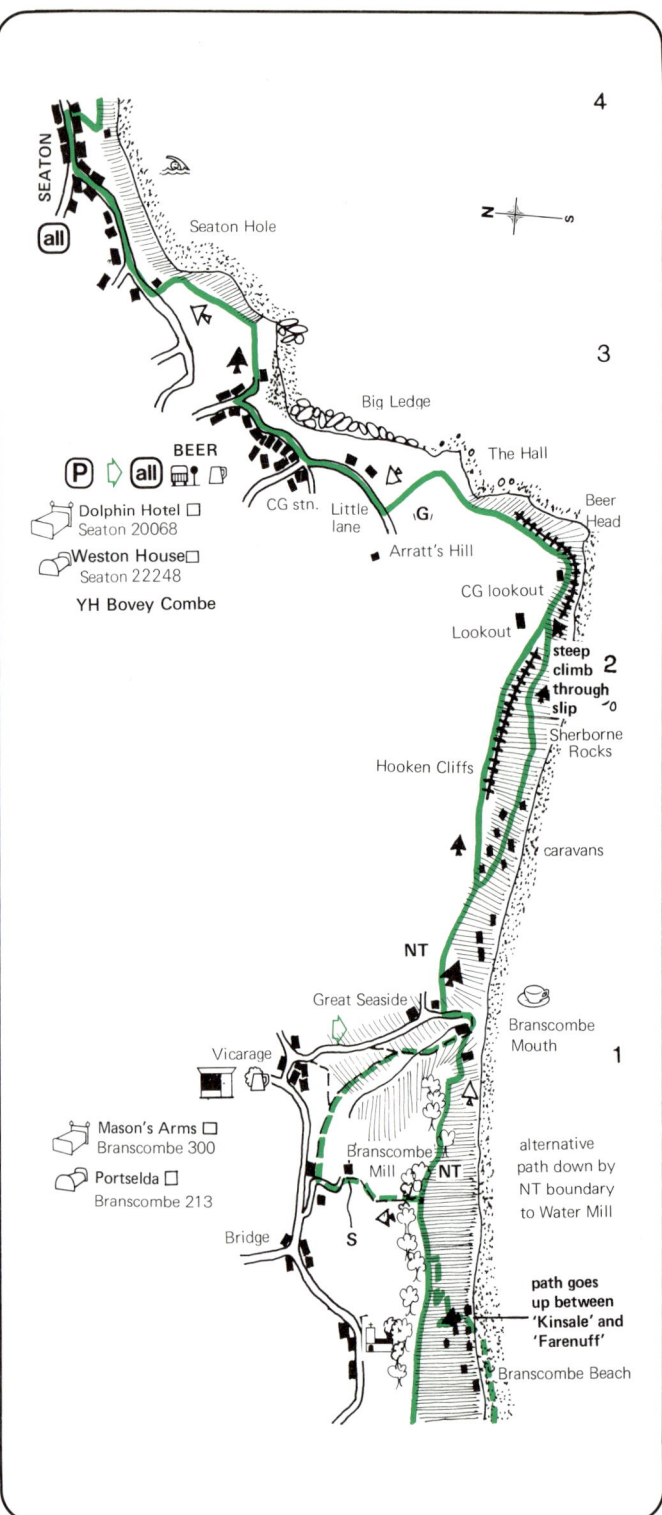

SEATON

Seaton Hole

4

N

3

Big Ledge

The Hall

BEER

Beer Head

P ⇨ **all** 🍴🍺

Dolphin Hotel ☐
Seaton 20068

Weston House ☐
Seaton 22248

YH Bovey Combe

CG stn. Little **G**
lane

Arratt's Hill

CG lookout

Lookout

**steep
climb
through
slip**

2

Sherborne
Rocks

Hooken Cliffs

caravans

NT

Great Seaside

Branscombe
Mouth

1

Vicarage

Mason's Arms ☐
Branscombe 300

Portselda ☐
Branscombe 213

Branscombe
Mill

NT

alternative
path down by
NT boundary
to Water Mill

Bridge

S

**path goes
up between
'Kinsale' and
'Farenuff'**

Branscombe Beach

23 Branscombe Beach-Beer-Seaton

4 miles 6½km From Plymouth 107 miles 172km

Going: you have a choice of two paths on leaving Branscombe Beach. You can walk over the 400ft Hooken Cliff or take an undercliff route through the Under Hooken landslip. Both are quite strenuous. After that, there is good uncomplicated cliff walking down to Beer and over to Seaton.

Branscombe is regarded deservedly as one of the most attractive villages in south Devon. It is really a collection of houses, most of them very old, strung along 2 miles of road, through a green and smiling valley. Its name is of Celtic origin, and records go back for more than 1000 years. King Alfred owned the manor during his reign and it was then given by King Athelstan to the monastery, later the Cathedral, of Exeter in 995. The church has traces of its Saxon origin and many features of interest including a mediaeval wall-painting. Opposite the church is a house known as Church Living where visiting clerics used to stay, parts of which are 700 years old. Farther down the road are thatched cottages, a forge, an old bakery, and a pub— the Mason's Arms, built out of old cottages. A booklet is on sale in the church, which gives many facts of interest on the village and its surroundings.

From near the Mason's Arms, a footpath leads along the stream to the shore and the Coast Path. Great Seaside, near the mouth of the valley, is a farmhouse from Tudor times.

From Branscombe Mouth, there are two alternative routes on the way to Beer: one climbs up the imposing slope of Hooken Cliff, along the almost flat top and down the other side. For the other, you take the private road through the collection of bungalows close to the shore (there is a right-of-way for walkers). The road soon becomes a footpath. The Path winds its way through the bumps, hollows and thick vegetation of the undercliff. This is the earliest (in modern times) of the famous landslips on this part of the coast. In March 1790, 10 acres of land broke away from the cliff into hundreds of tons of chalk boulders, pushing back the shore line 200yds. The landslip is of interest to naturalists and the caves, uncovered high in the cliffs, are appreciated by climbers (don't try yourself; it needs experience).

The two paths join at the top of Hooken Cliff and continue, past the Coast Guard lookout, round Beer Head, a chalk cliff—in fact, the westermost chalk outcrop in the British Isles. There is evidence of Neolithic flint workings here. From Beer Head, you continue through fields, turning inland through a kissing-gate (caravan site on left) to join Little Lane. Past the Coast Guard station, with its flag-staff, and down Common Hill to Beer, an attractive former fishing village.

The Path continues through the ornamental gardens above the small beach and brings you soon to Seaton.

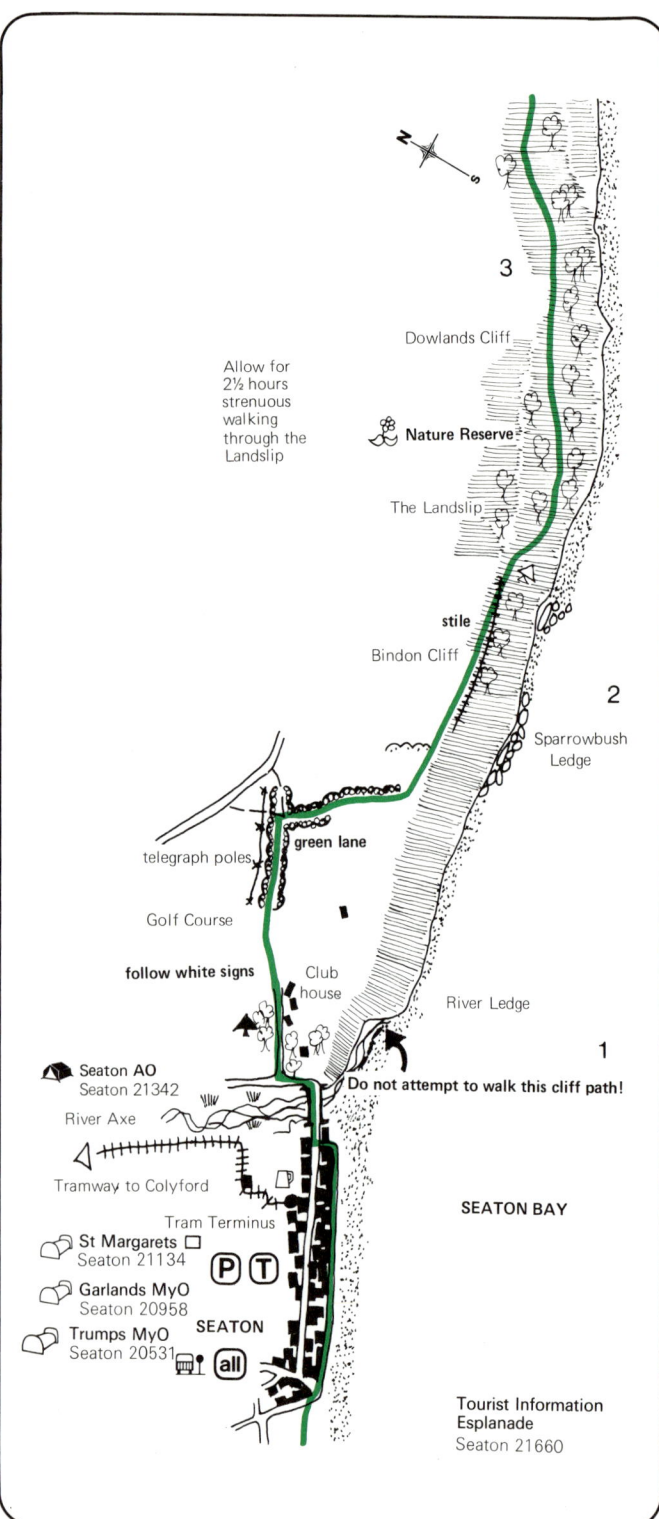

Allow for
2½ hours
strenuous
walking
through the
Landslip

Dowlands Cliff

Nature Reserve

The Landslip

stile

Bindon Cliff

Sparrowbush
Ledge

telegraph poles

green lane

Golf Course

follow white signs

Club
house

River Ledge

3

2

1

Seaton AO
Seaton 21342

River Axe

Do not attempt to walk this cliff path!

Tramway to Colyford

Tram Terminus

St Margarets ☐
Seaton 21134

Garlands MyO
Seaton 20958

Trumps MyO
Seaton 20531

SEATON

P **T**

all

SEATON BAY

**Tourist Information
Esplanade**
Seaton 21660

24 Seaton-Dowlands Landslip

3¾ miles 6km From Plymouth 110 miles 178km

Going: this section brings you half-way through the famous Landslip which stretches for 5 of the 6 miles between Seaton and Lyme Regis. Except for 1 mile at the east (Lyme Regis) end where it is wider, over most of its length, the Path is a narrow one which twists and turns, dips and climbs, through the nearest thing to a virgin forest you are likely to see in the British Isles. The Path becomes muddy and very slippery in wet weather. In any case, only those who are active and reasonably sure-footed should attempt to walk right through. The only access for the public is at each end. Take with you any refreshments you may need as there are no facilities en route. Leaflets on the Landslip can be had from the Information Bureau on the front in Seaton or from the council offices.

Seaton (population 4200) a popular small resort with a shelving shingle beach. From Roman remains found nearby, Seaton may have been the site of a Roman port but in later times it was better known for its smuggling activities. John Rattenbury, the most famous smuggler in the area, is buried in the churchyard. The Seaton Electric Tramway is run by a private company which has taken over the British Rail line that runs along the Axe. Sub-size trams run to Colyford and Colyton.

From the east end of the Promenade in Seaton you can join the main road which takes the bridge across the river Axe. A few yards up the road, on the right, is the drive leading to the Axe Cliff Golf Club. The Coast Path follows this drive and is well sign-posted, past the Club House and across a part of the course, entering a lane through a field gate. Follow this lane, between hedges, until you come to a sign on the right directing you over fields. This Path will bring you, across two stiles, to the entrance of the Landslip, a National Nature Reserve since 1955. In the Reserve keep to the marked path; you cannot visit parts away from the path without a permit. Details from the Nature Conservancy, Roughmoor, Bishop's Hull, Taunton.

The Reserve is of intense interest to geologists and naturalists. The whole Landslip area, 5 miles long and ½ mile wide, has been caused by the collapse of the cliff structure. The most sensational landslip occurred on Christmas Eve 1839 when 20 acres (roughly the 3rd mile of this section) subsided. The landslips were apparently caused by the collapse, through waterlogging, of porous chalk and other strata, above a more solid limestone layer which sloped towards the sea. The rocks of the Reserve abound in fossils. From a natural history point of view the chief interest lies in the vegetation, the trees and plants having grown without human interference or influence. The grove of ash trees is unique and there is an unusual profusion and variety of plants. Over 100 species of birds, resident and migrant, have been identified in the Reserve; it is one of the few places in the south-west where the nightingale breeds.

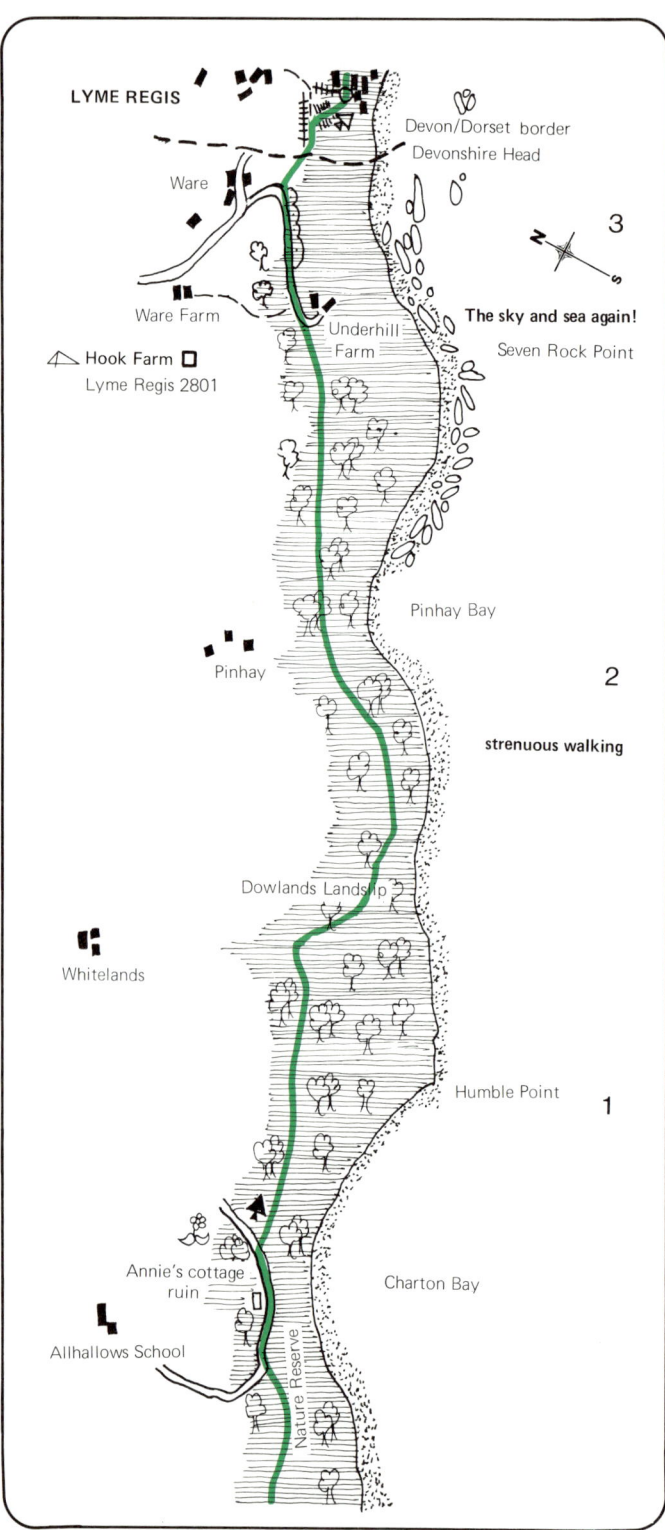

LYME REGIS

Ware

Ware Farm

Devon/Dorset border
Devonshire Head

The sky and sea again!

Seven Rock Point

Underhill
Farm

△ **Hook Farm** ▢
Lyme Regis 2801

Pinhay Bay

Pinhay

2

strenuous walking

Dowlands Landslip

Whitelands

Humble Point

1

Annie's cottage
ruin

Charton Bay

Allhallows School

Nature Reserve

3

N

25 Dowlands Landslip-Lyme Regis

3½ miles 5½km From Plymouth 113½ miles 183½km

Going: this section covers the east half of the Landslip Nature Reserve and the remarks given under the previous section also apply to this. The Devon/Dorset border is just beyond the Landslip. You are now in Dorset.

On emerging from the Landslip you follow a farm track above Underhill Farm and then a signposted Path diagonally across fields which brings you out to a car-park above the Cobb.

Lyme Regis (population 3500) is a resort with a long history. Its famous harbour, the Cobb, is believed to date from the 14th century. Mentioned in the Domesday Book, Lyme was granted a charter in 1284 and regularly contributed ships and men in times of emergency including the Armada. The ill-fated Duke of Monmouth landed here in 1685 to start his rebellion. Many Lyme citizens who joined him shared his fate and were executed.

One of Lyme's best known personalities was Mary Anning, the poor girl, orphaned when she was 10, whose only means of livelihood was the selling of fossils she found in the neighbourhood. She became so famous that geologists from all over the world used to write to her for specimens. She was granted a Government pension until she died in 1847. The fossils of the ichthyosaurus, previously unknown, one of them 21ft long, were found by her in the landslip areas of Dowlands and Back Ven (section 26). Some of them are in the British Museum (Natural History) and the Geological Museum. The Philpot Museum in Lyme contains much of interest, historical and geological. In the nearby Information Bureau and in the Museum leaflets on the Landslip are obtainable.

Lyme Regis must be unique in the number of visitors, both young and old, seen walking about with geological hammers!

There is the old pub, the Royal Standard, on the Cobb.

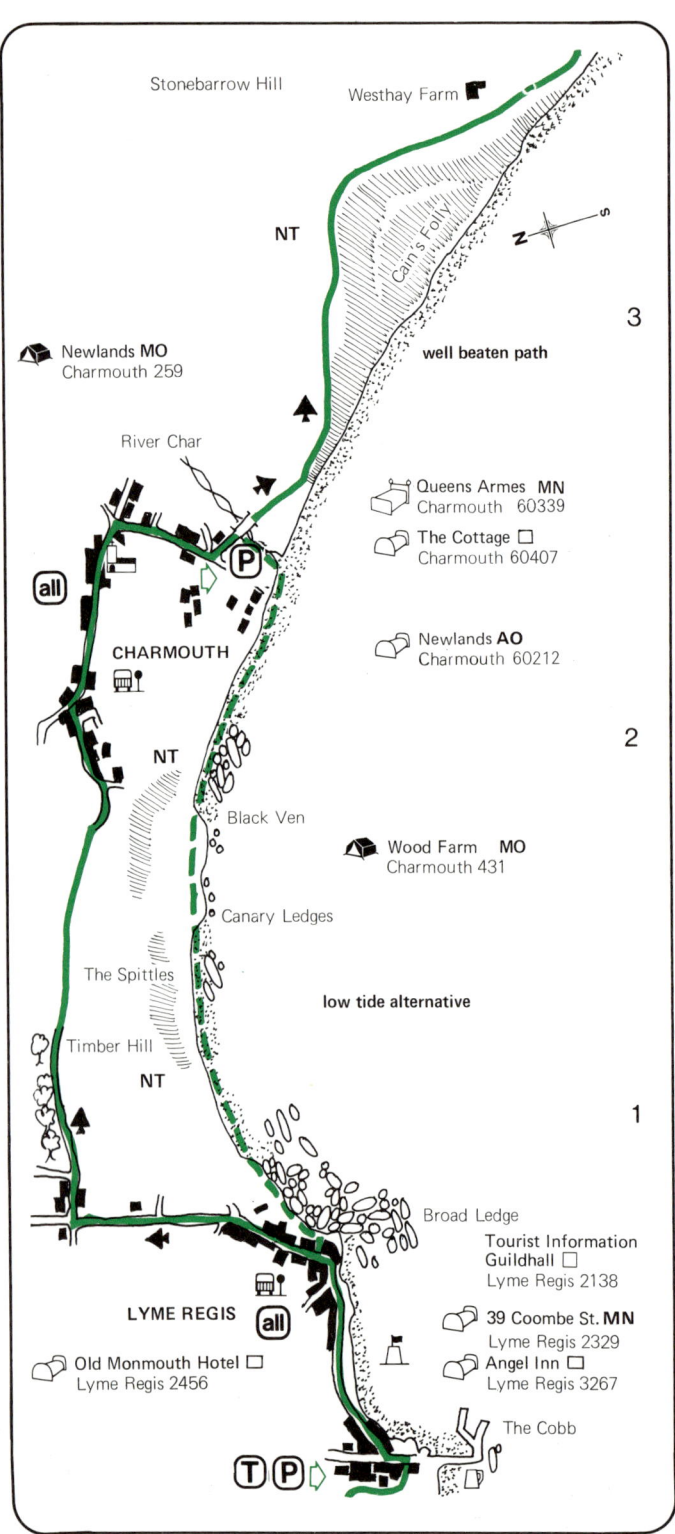

Stonebarrow Hill

Westhay Farm

NT

Cain's Folly

N

S

3

Newlands **MO**
Charmouth 259

well beaten path

River Char

Queens Armes **MN**
Charmouth 60339

The Cottage □
Charmouth 60407

all

Newlands **AO**
Charmouth 60212

CHARMOUTH

2

NT

Black Ven

Wood Farm **MO**
Charmouth 431

Canary Ledges

The Spittles

low tide alternative

Timber Hill

NT

1

Broad Ledge

Tourist Information
Guildhall □
Lyme Regis 2138

LYME REGIS

all

39 Coombe St. **MN**
Lyme Regis 2329

Old Monmouth Hotel □
Lyme Regis 2456

Angel Inn □
Lyme Regis 3267

The Cobb

T P

60

26 Lyme Regis-Charmouth-Stonebarrow Hill

3¾ miles 6km From Plymouth 117¼ miles 189½km

Going: a climb along the main road out of Lyme Regis; a cliff walk to Charmouth and then a pull up the long slope of Stonebarrow Hill. We recommend that, if the tide is right, you walk along the beach all the way to Charmouth.

From the centre of Lyme Regis take the main Charmouth Road (A3052) which climbs steeply out of the town. After about 1 mile there is a turning on the right which, after passing some houses, ascends as a track past a wood to the top of Timber Hill. A path continues along the boundary of the Golf Course, coming out eventually on the cliff-edge, above Black Ven, a wild expanse of gorse and bramble between the cliff and the sea.

Black Ven is another landslip area and is a Nature Reserve to which there is no public access. It was in Black Ven where the 12-year-old Mary Anning found the 21ft fossil of the ichthyosaurus, now in the British Museum (Natural History).

On these cliffs, in the 18th century and again earlier in this century, there have been spontaneous fires, the earth bursting into flame, in the same way as at Burning Cliff (section 34).

The cliff-top path eventually leads to a lane which emerges on the road, Old Lyme Hill, running down into Charmouth. As mentioned above, it is preferable to walk on the beach between Lyme and Charmouth.

Charmouth (population 1000): a former fishing village, the site of battles between Saxon and Dane in the 9th century. In the Civil War its sympathies were on the Parliamentary side. Charles II, fleeing in disguise after the battle of Worcester in 1651, stayed at The Queens Armes in Charmouth while arranging with a local skipper to be taken to France. The skipper's wife became suspicious and, not wishing her husband to risk execution, hid his trousers. The King had to leave quickly and eventually escaped from Brighton.

To regain the Coast Path take the turning on the right coming down the hill, past the Church. This is Lower Sea Lane. Almost at the end of this lane there is a footpath on the left leading to a footbridge over the river Char. Cross this footbridge and you are on the green turf of the lower slopes of Stonebarrow Hill. A well-walked path leads to the crest of this 500ft cliff.

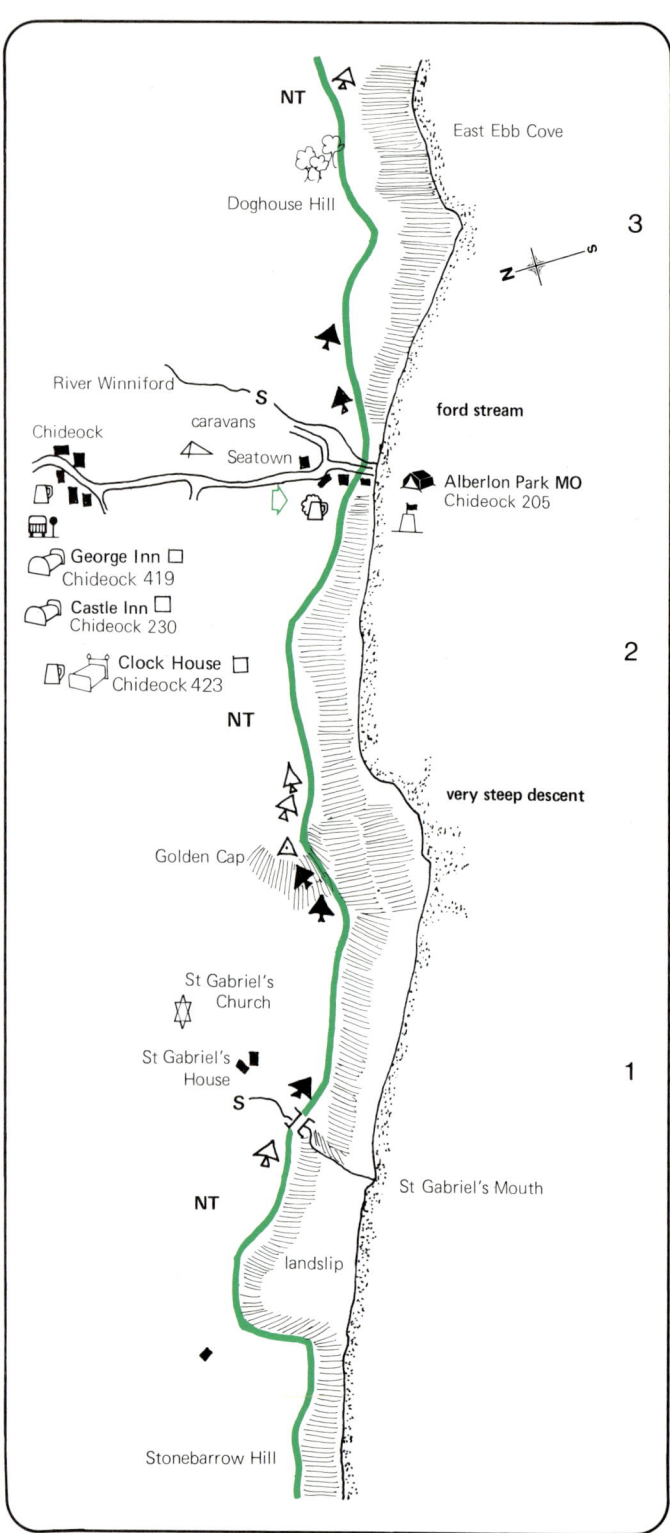

NT

East Ebb Cove

Doghouse Hill

3

N S

River Winniford

S

caravans

ford stream

Chideock

Seatown

Alberlon Park **MO**
Chideock 205

George Inn □
Chideock 419

Castle Inn □
Chideock 230

Clock House □
Chideock 423

2

NT

very steep descent

Golden Cap

St Gabriel's
Church

St Gabriel's
House

1

S

St Gabriel's Mouth

NT

landslip

◆

Stonebarrow Hill

62

27 Stonebarrow Hill-Seatown-East Ebb Cove

3½ miles 5½km From Plymouth 120¾ miles 195km

Going: a fine stretch of cliff walking, in open country with fine views. A succession of steep gradients, particularly up Golden Cap.

On the top of Stonebarrow Hill is the west boundary of a fine expanse of National Trust coast property and, as one comes to expect and appreciate, there is a good stile and a signpost, in this case telling you it's 2 hours walking to Eype (pronounced: eep). The Path follows as close as possible the line of the cliffs with wonderful wide vistas: inland, of rolling field and woodland; seaward, of Lyme Bay fringed by its towering but graceful cliffs.

In the first dip is the substantial farmstead of St Gabriel, in a perfect setting. On the slope opposite is the ruin of the 700-year-old chapel of St Gabriel from which it takes its name.

An acre of land here, St Gabriels Bank, is a Nature Reserve of the Dorset Naturalist Trust, the object being the preservation of its wild flowers.

The Path keeps to the cliff-edge up the slope of the 612ft Golden Cap. This is the highest point on the whole of the south Coast and the last part of the climb is pretty steep, as are the first few yards of the descent the other side. The name is said to be derived from the yellowish colour of the Lias (Jurassic limestone) of the cliff in certain light conditions.

The lower slopes are gentler and bring you gradually down to the little hamlet of Seatown with the very welcome Anchor pub by the water's edge and a beach to relax on. The next climb is up Doghouse Hill to Thorncombe Beacon, above East Ebb Cove.

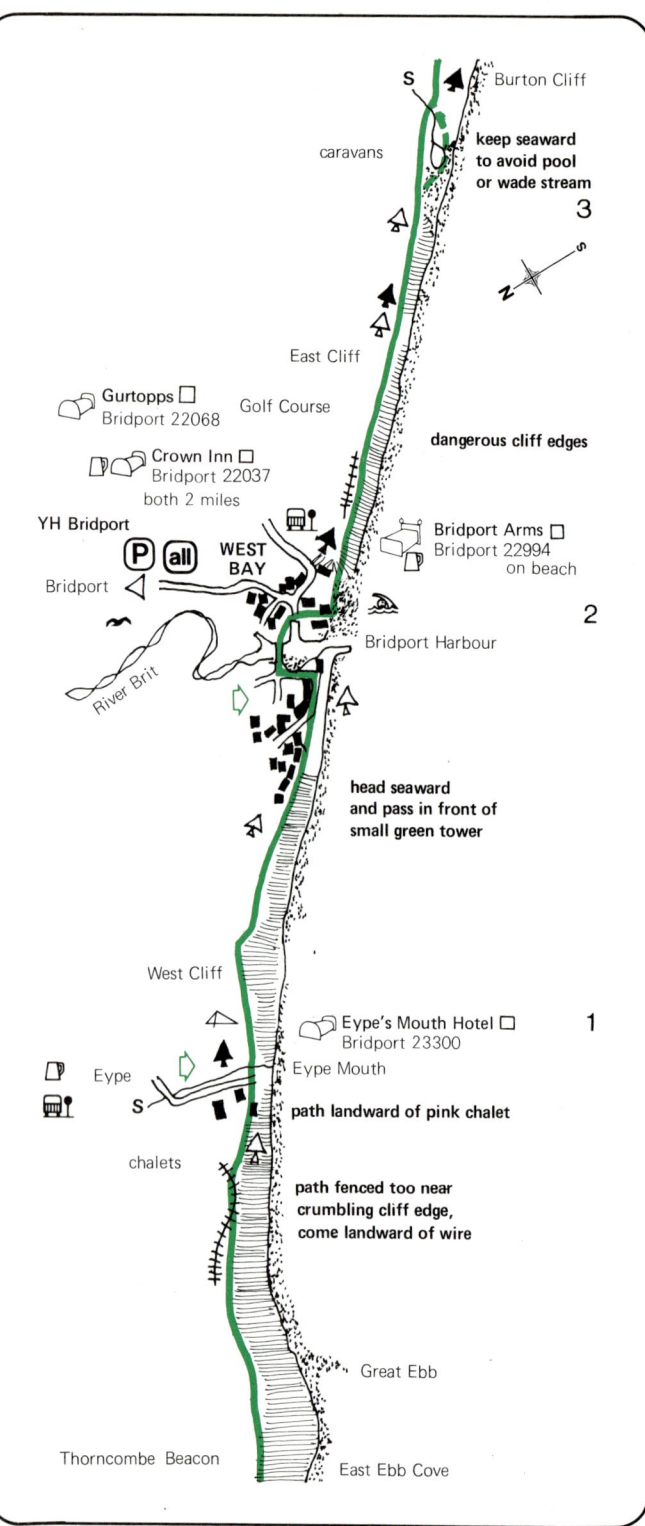

S Burton Cliff

keep seaward
to avoid pool
or wade stream

caravans

3

East Cliff

Gurtopps
Bridport 22068   Golf Course

Crown Inn
Bridport 22037
both 2 miles

YH Bridport

dangerous cliff edges

P all   WEST
BAY

Bridport

Bridport Arms
Bridport 22994
on beach

2

River Brit

Bridport Harbour

head seaward
and pass in front of
small green tower

West Cliff

Eype's Mouth Hotel
Bridport 23300

1

Eype   Eype Mouth

S   path landward of pink chalet

chalets

path fenced too near
crumbling cliff edge,
come landward of wire

Great Ebb

Thorncombe Beacon   East Ebb Cove

28 East Ebb Cove-West Bay-Burton Cliff

3½ miles 5½km From Plymouth 124¼ miles 200½km
Going: an undemanding stretch, with two moderate cliff climbs.

From Thorncombe Beacon above East Ebb Cove, a gentle descent to Eype Mouth—just a car-park and a hut or two, with a shingle beach.

The village of Eype, with two pubs, is ½ mile up the road running inland.

On the slope of West Cliff, on the other side of the small stream, is a caravan and camp site. The Path climbs West Cliff, keeping near the edge, and then, down past a line of bungalows, to West Bay.

West Bay, a small port and resort, with an extensive caravan and camping site, was known before 1884, when the railway came, as Bridport Harbour. The first harbour piers were built in the 14th century the chief activity being the export of ropes, cordage, and nets which were the main products of the town of Bridport, 2 miles inland up the river Brit (the wide streets of Bridport were needed for rope making). The introduction of the steamship brought a decline to West Bay but there is still a small fishing fleet and a few timber boats from abroad using the harbour, as well as the many sailing dinghies and other pleasure craft so popular nowadays. There are all facilities for refreshment and accommodation.

On the east side of the harbour the Path ascends the low East Cliff, along the edge of the Golf Course. On the other side of East Cliff is a huge caravan and camping site. You can either keep to the shore and cross the stream if the water level allows you to use the stepping stones, or take the footpath inland along the west bank of the stream, round the outskirts of the caravan site, which brings you over a footbridge to Burton Bradstock, well worth a visit (see next section).

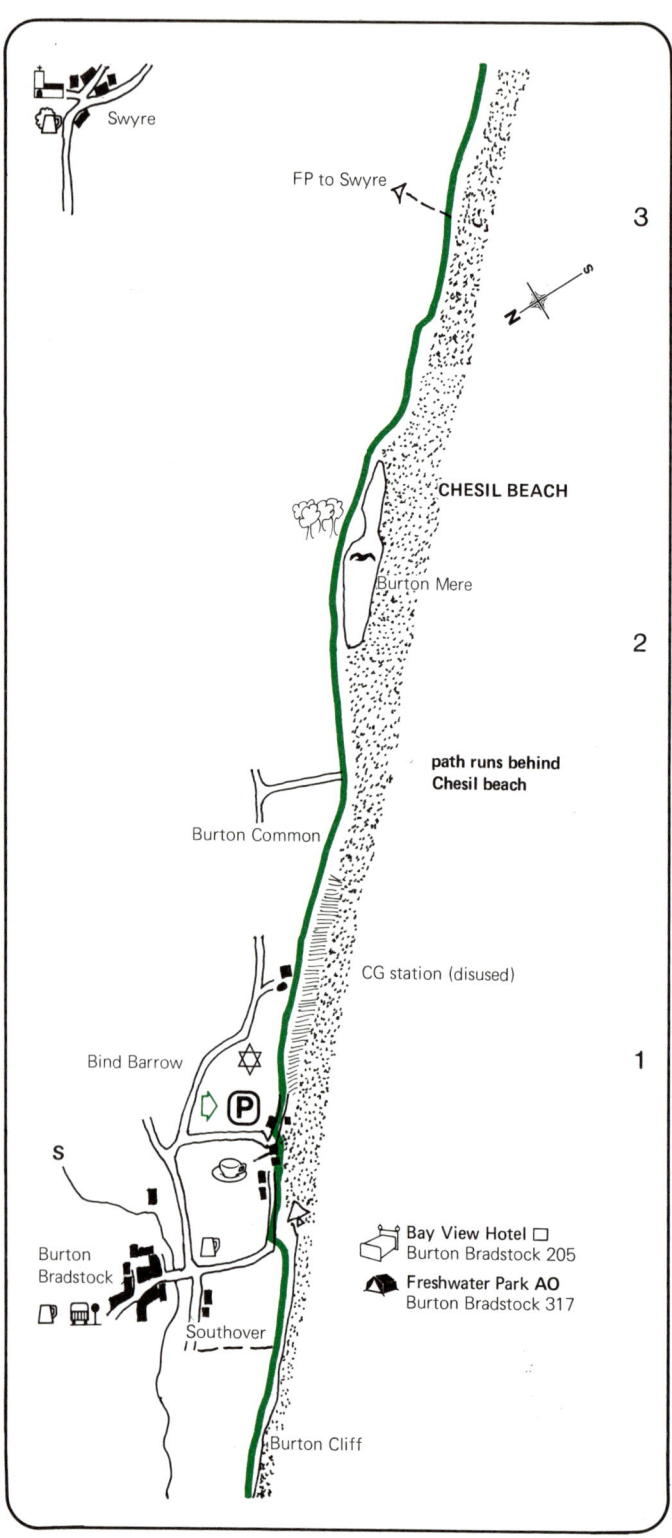

Swyre

FP to Swyre

3

CHESIL BEACH

Burton Mere

2

path runs behind
Chesil beach

Burton Common

CG station (disused)

Bind Barrow

1

P

S

Bay View Hotel □
Burton Bradstock 205

Freshwater Park AO
Burton Bradstock 317

Burton
Bradstock

Southover

Burton Cliff

29 Burton Cliff-Swyre (Chesil Beach)

3½ miles 5½km From Plymouth 127¾ miles 206km

Going: for this section and the next the Coast Path runs behind the renowned Chesil Beach, the monotony of which can be relieved by the observation of wild life.

On the coast opposite the village of Burton Bradstock you have the low yellow sandstone Burton Cliffs. A cliff fall as recent as February 1976 has deposited many tons of rock on the shore, of which many fossil-hunters have taken advantage.

Burton Bradstock is one of Dorset's most charming villages and well worth the short detour necessary for a visit, particularly outside the months of July and August when it tends to be flooded by visitors from the large Holiday Park nearby. Mentioned in the Domesday Book, Burton Bradstock takes its name from the Priory of Bradenstoke in Wiltshire to whom the manor was presented in the 12th century. It has an ancient church, thatched cottages, and some delightful 17th century houses. There is also Mill Street leading to the church with an old flax mill which was used for spinning locally grown flax for ropes and nets. The other main occupation was fishing, with 14 pubs catering for the fishermen's thirst—today reduced to three, who do their best to deal with the wants of the mackerel boats that survive. Pubs: the Dove, Anchor and Three Horseshoes.

The Path is routed along Burton Cliff and when the cliff gives way to Chesil Beach, proceeds for the next 7 miles behind this formidable shingle barrier. There is a slight diversion inland at Burton Mere.

Chesil Beach is an 18 mile bank of shingle about 200yds wide and about 50ft high, thrown up by the tide over thousands of years. One curious feature is that the pebbles of the Beach get regularly smaller the farther west you go: at the Portland (east) end they are over 3in; at the Burton end they are the size of a pea. One theory is that the waves sort them out in sizes but as Derrick Knowlton points out in The Naturalist in Central Southern England, *one cannot understand why this does not happen to other shingle beaches. The Beach is particularly menacing in stormy weather and has been responsible for hundreds of shipwrecks. One 500 ton ship was blown clean over the bank in the 1820s, and there have been some disastrous floods, right up to recent times. Bathing is always dangerous, as is boating. The marshy Burton Mere encountered on this section is a refuge for wildfowl, particularly in spring, autumn, and winter.*

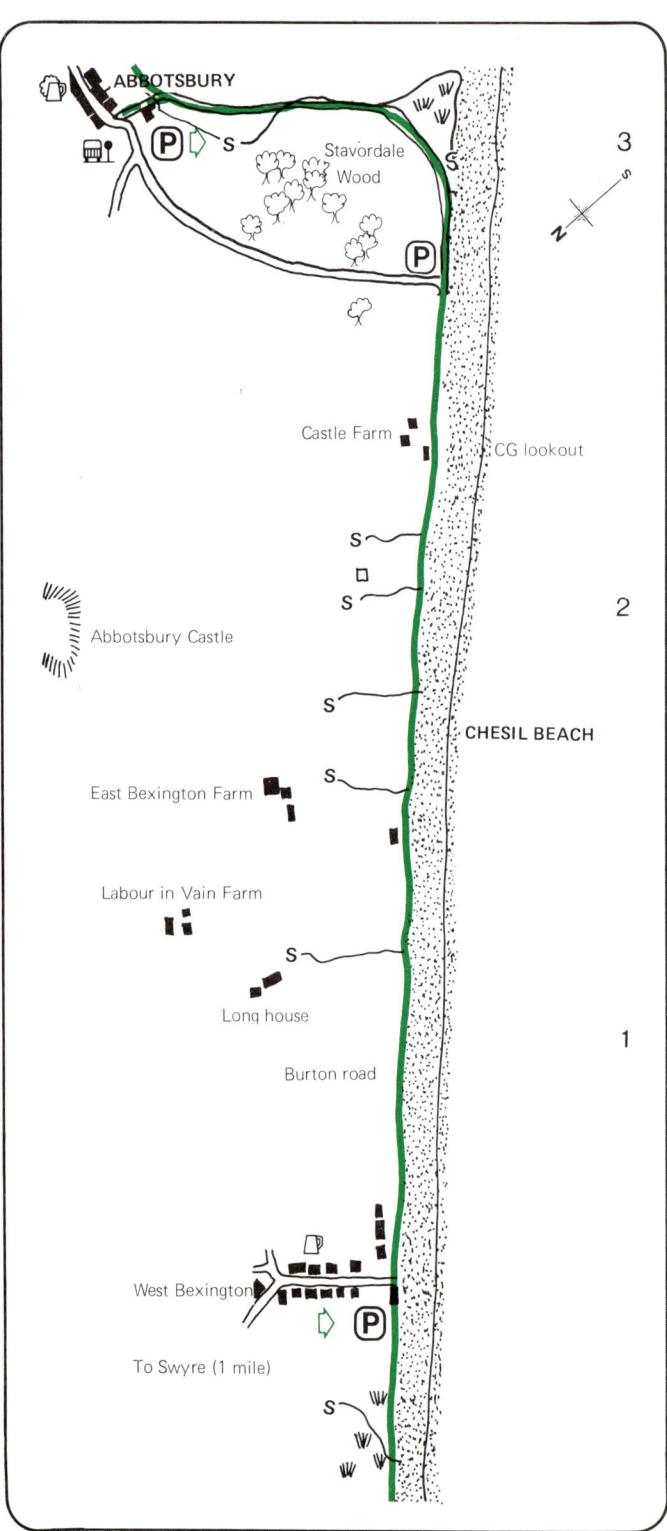

ABBOTSBURY

Stavordale Wood

S

S

3

Castle Farm

CG lookout

S

S

Abbotsbury Castle

S

2

CHESIL BEACH

East Bexington Farm

S

Labour in Vain Farm

S

Long house

1

Burton road

West Bexington

To Swyre (1 mile)

S

30 Swyre (Chesil Beach)-Abbotsbury
3¾ miles 6km   From Plymouth 131½ miles 212km
Going: the Path continues in a straight line behind Chesil Beach for another 3 miles and then turns inland to Abbotsbury.

Continuing behind the Beach you come to where a road from West Bexington reaches the Beach. The village is ½ mile inland and has a post office and pub, the Manor House.

2½ miles beyond the West Bexington Road you arrive at the Coast Guard lookout which is linked by road to Abbotsbury. The Path is along this road until it turns inland. Here there is a space where cars are parked; in the landward corner of this space is a stile with a Coast Path sign, the start of a pleasant farm track leading to Abbotsbury.

On the slopes of the meadow to the left (west) of the Path can clearly be seen the lines of the mediaeval 'strip' cultivation of the fields.

In Abbotsbury (see next section) and the area immediately surrounding the village—including, no doubt, the fields, woods and streams we can see here from the Path—you have probably the best preserved evidence anywhere in the country of countryside dominated in the Middle Ages by a powerful Abbey. There must have been dozens of similar monastic estates before the Dissolution in the 16th century.

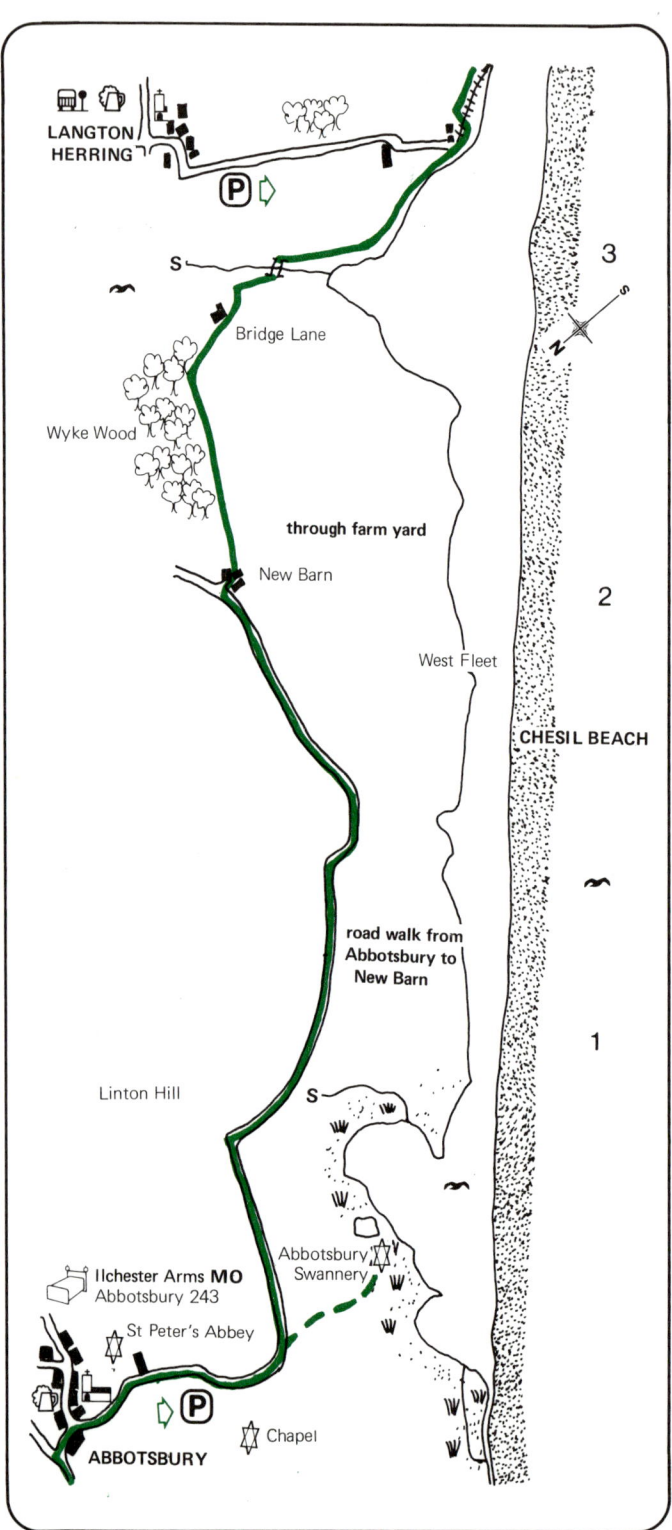

LANGTON
HERRING

P

S

Bridge Lane

Wyke Wood

through farm yard

New Barn

West Fleet

3

CHESIL BEACH

2

1

road walk from
Abbotsbury to
New Barn

Linton Hill

S

Ilchester Arms **MO**
Abbotsbury 243

St Peter's Abbey

Abbotsbury
Swannery

P

Chapel

ABBOTSBURY

31 Abbotsbury-Langton Herring

3¾ miles 6km   From Plymouth 135¼ miles 218km

Going: after Abbotsbury—well worth a visit—and until a footpath is ready, you have to walk for 2 miles along the road to New Barn. From New Barn field paths take you back to the coast.

Abbotsbury deservedly attracts many visitors who are charmed by the houses built from local stone, and the remaining buildings of the famous Benedictine house of Abbotsbury whose foundation goes back to the time of King Canute. Of the Abbey itself little remains, but the great stone 14th-century Barn, 90yds long, gives a good idea of the prosperity of the Abbey in the Middle Ages. Equally impressive is St Catherine's Chapel crowning the 200ft Chapel Hill just outside the village. This massive 14th-century chapel building with walls 4ft thick has stone roof vaulting, an unusual refinement. The Chapel may have been primarily to serve as a landmark for shipping. It can be visited. The church of St Peter in the village is 16th century with earlier parts. There is a list of vicars going back for over 600 years.

The Abbotsbury Swannery which has been there since the 16th century can be visited May-September. It lies at the end of a turning off the road to New Barn. 500 mute swans use the Swannery which is the largest breeding place for them in the country. They can be seen on their nests in May. They range quite a way from the Swannery and can be observed on the Fleet, the stretch of brackish water extending behind Chesil Beach from Abbotsbury to Weymouth, along which our Coast Path runs on the next two sections.

After walking the 2 miles along the road to New Barn, join the Path by going through the yard of the farm and along the edge of Wyke Wood—where you may see warblers, blackcaps, and redstarts in the spring.

Emerging from the Wood the Path proceeds across the field in front of the farmhouse marked on the map as Bridge Lane, to a stile (signpost). Across another field and over a footbridge, the route turns seaward, coming out on the bank of the Fleet. Although the OS map shows the right-of-way as cutting inland slightly here, there is no trace of the Path. Better to keep to the edge of the water until you come to the end of the road which leads inland to Langton Herring.

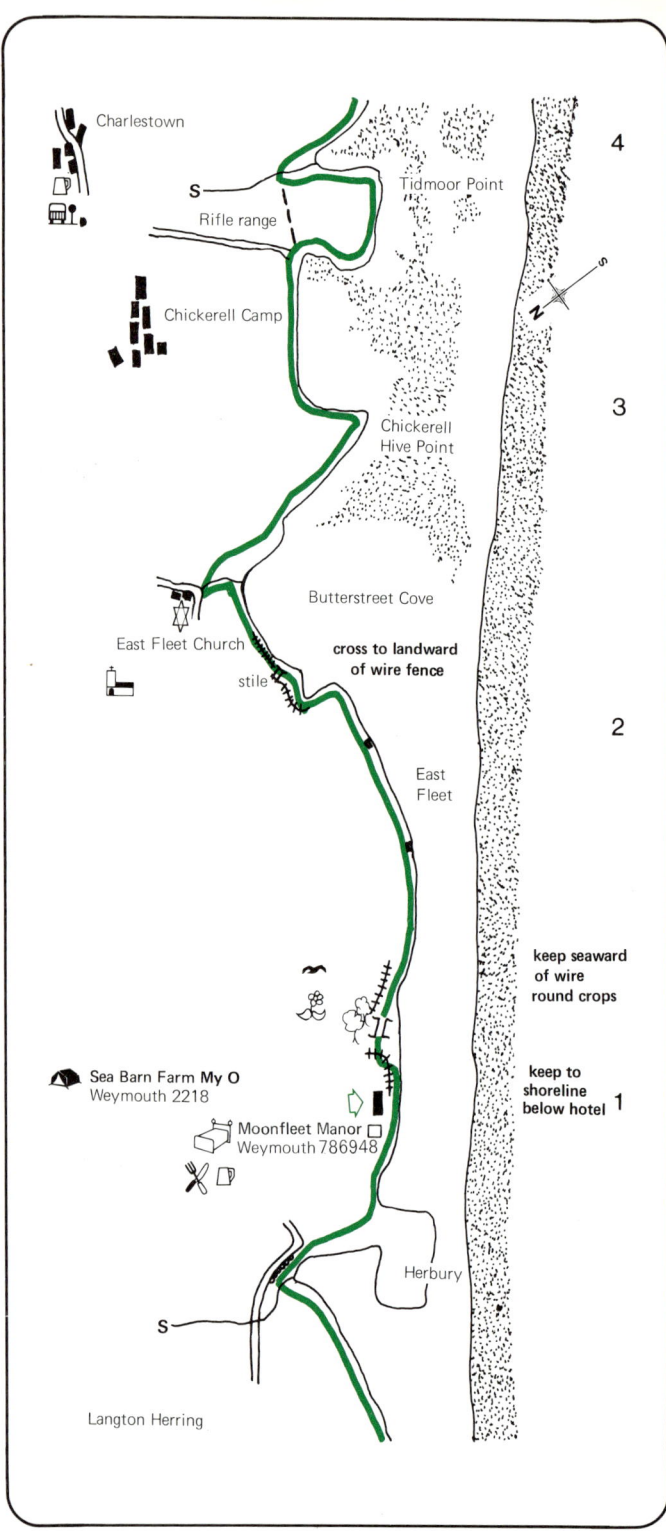

Charlestown

S

Rifle range

Tidmoor Point

Chickerell Camp

Chickerell
Hive Point

Butterstreet Cove

**cross to landward
of wire fence**

East Fleet Church

stile

East
Fleet

**keep seaward
of wire
round crops**

🏕 **Sea Barn Farm My O**
Weymouth 2218

**keep to
shoreline
below hotel**

⬜ **Moonfleet Manor** ☐
Weymouth 786948

Herbury

S

Langton Herring

4

N
S

3

2

1

32 Langton Herring-Charlestown

4¼ miles 7km   From Plymouth 139½ miles 225km

Going: by field path along the edge of the Fleet—a quiet, lonely, scene but with much of natural history interest.

Langton Herring, a small, beautifully situated village, 1 mile up the road from the Fleet, reached at the end of the previous section, has a good pub—the Elm Tree, which has a well patronized restaurant. Herring has nothing to do with fishing; it is the name of the Lords of the Manor in the Middle Ages. If you have made the detour inland to Langton Herring you will find a signposted track south of the Elm Tree which runs pleasantly down to the bank of the Fleet and the Coast Path.

The Path continues along the bank of the Fleet and cuts across the neck of the small promontory, Herbury. We then come to the Moonfleet Hotel. Moonfleet is the scene of the novel of the same name by J M Falkner.

The Moonfleet Hotel incorporates a pub, the Mohun Arms, if you need a drink and something to eat.

Parts of Chesil Beach, including the Fleet, are a local Nature Reserve, for its flora and bird-life. The Abbotsbury swans feed on the eel-grass; in the spring and early summer common and little terns may be seen—they have a protected nesting site.

The landscape inland from the Path here is quite undulating. On a 200ft hill is a Fleet Air Arm helicopter station. Pleasant meadowland runs down to the Fleet and there is always the unusual bird or wild flower to watch out for.

You next come, at East Fleet, to a line of picturesque cottages and a small ancient church, or, rather, all that was left of it after a storm in 1824 which also decimated the village. Still hugging the shore of the Fleet the Path rounds another small promontory which is used as an army shooting range. Red flags indicate when firing is taking place; at such times you can carry straight on across the neck of the promontory. When there is no firing you can walk round it.

From the range a track inland brings you to the main road B3157 at Charlestown from which there is a bus service for the 2 miles into the centre of Weymouth; if you prefer, the Path continues to Weymouth, mainly past built-up areas, round the shore of Portland Harbour. This route is described in the Section dealing with Weymouth in the Appendix.

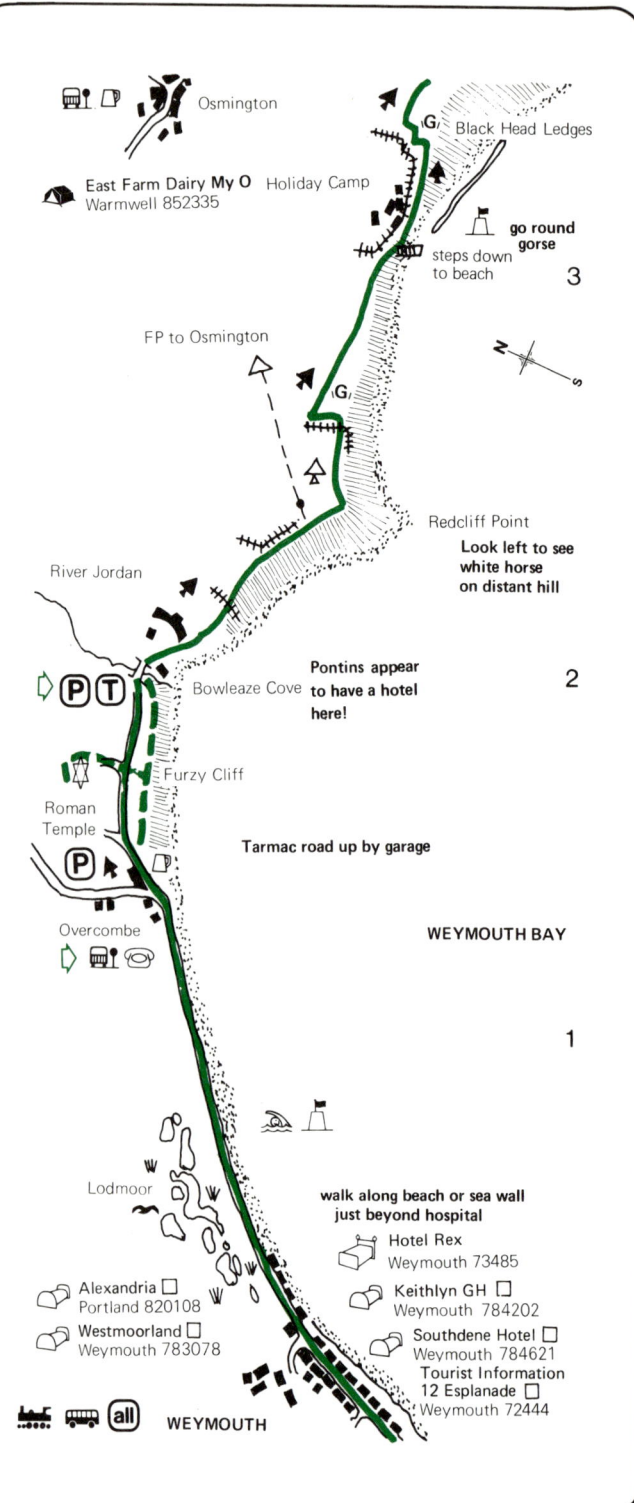

Osmington

East Farm Dairy **My O**
Warmwell 852335 Holiday Camp

G Black Head Ledges

go round gorse

steps down to beach

3

FP to Osmington

G

Redcliff Point

Look left to see white horse on distant hill

River Jordan

P T

Bowleaze Cove **Pontins appear to have a hotel here!**

2

Furzy Cliff

Roman Temple

P

Tarmac road up by garage

Overcombe

WEYMOUTH BAY

1

Lodmoor

walk along beach or sea wall just beyond hospital

Hotel Rex
Weymouth 73485

Alexandria ☐
Portland 820108

Keithlyn GH ☐
Weymouth 784202

Westmoorland ☐
Weymouth 783078

Southdene Hotel ☐
Weymouth 784621
Tourist Information
12 Esplanade ☐
Weymouth 72444

all **WEYMOUTH**

33 Weymouth-Black Head

3¾ miles 6km   From Plymouth 147¼ miles 237¼km

Going: the first 1½ miles is along the main road, then good cliff walking.

You can either walk along the coastal main road for 1½ miles or take a 413 bus which runs quite frequently from 'the Statue', the gay coloured figure of the town's benefactor George III, on the seafront. Ask for Overcombe. At Overcombe take the road up past the garage (there is a signpost to the Jordan Hill Roman Temple). From the pub car-park go over Furzy Cliff, on the crest of which you get a fine view inland of George III on his White Horse. On the left of the road is the Jordan Hill Roman Temple.

Only the foundations of the Roman Temple remain. It was discovered in 1843; an urn of Roman coins was unearthed at the same time. The Roman road from the important city of Dunovaria (Dorchester) reached the coast only 2 miles away, so in Roman times there must have been a bit of activity here— remains of a villa have been found nearby at Preston.

The road leads down to the mouth of the river Jordan, the whole scene being dominated by a large holiday hotel. The Coast Path leads up the cliff on the seaward side of the hotel, and you are soon out on open downland with gorse bushes and with fine views.

Between the Path and the sea lies a wide expanse of gorse, bramble, and low trees, obviously covering an earlier landslip or a series of cliff falls. Such wild areas provide a fine landfall or jumping-off place for visiting birds on migration, so keep your eyes open if you are there in spring, early summer, or autumn. The Radipole marsh area just outside Weymouth is well known for its bird life.

In a wooded dip you come across another holiday complex which for once does not offend the eye or spoil the scene. The Path is signposted past the chalets and you soon come to the 250ft Black Head.

If you are planning to walk the Coast Path from Lulworth to Kimmeridge, check whether the route is open, as it is a military range (see Sections 36 and 37).

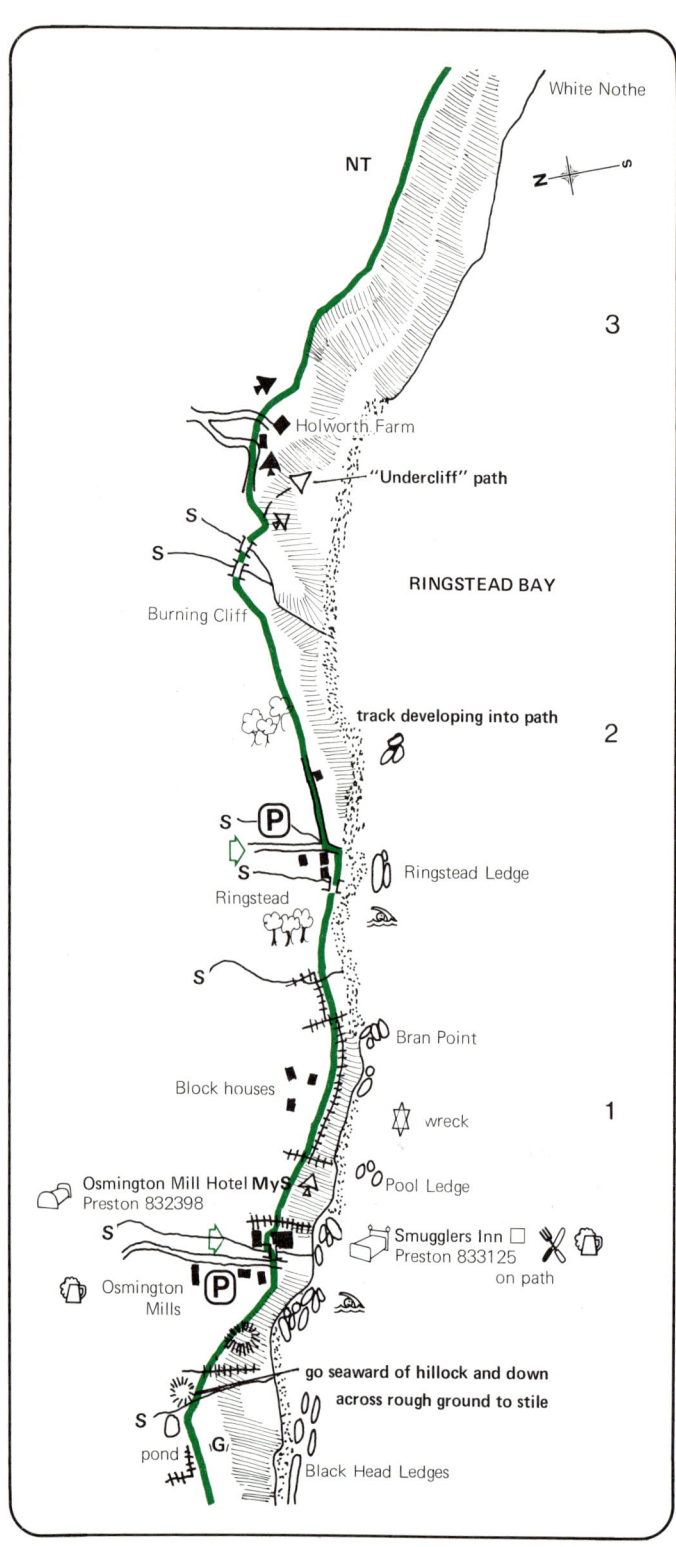

White Nothe

NT

3

Holworth Farm

"Undercliff" path

S

S

N

Burning Cliff

RINGSTEAD BAY

track developing into path

2

S P

S

Ringstead

Ringstead Ledge

S

Bran Point

Block houses

wreck

1

Osmington Mill Hotel MyS
Preston 832398

Pool Ledge

S

Smugglers Inn
Preston 833125
on path

Osmington
Mills

P

go seaward of hillock and down

across rough ground to stile

S

pond   G

Black Head Ledges

34 Black Head-Osmington Mills-White Nothe

3½ miles 5½km From Plymouth 150¾ miles 242¾km

Going: finding your way down to Osmington Mills can be a bit of a problem. Once past Osmington Mills you have a rich variety of scenery and good cliff walking.

After you have topped the rise at Black Head you are faced in the small valley below you by an apparently dense expanse of bramble, gorse, and reeds. Keep seaward of the green hillock which is the top of Black Head, and with care you will find the Path. It is signposted at the bottom of the valley but not apparently on Black Head. Again, when you come over the next rise and see Osmington Mills below, keep as close as you can to the seaward of the fields and this will bring you to the car park opposite the 15th century Smugglers Inn which looks as though it must have been originally one of the mills.

The Path continues through the garden (left-hand side) of the Smugglers Inn and up over the fields. You soon drop down almost to the water's edge before reaching the few bungalows and villas at Ringstead (no facilities). The steamer whose wreck you see is the *Minx* which was stranded on the rocks in 1929.

The original village of Ringstead has been 'lost'. ½ mile inland all that remains are a few banks and hollows in the grass where once were cottages and streets. The population may have been destroyed by the Black Death or in pirate raids—perhaps a combination of both.

You have to turn inland along the road for a few yards after passing the first line of bungalows. The Coast Path then follows a sign indicating a wide track on the right of the road. Once past a few more bungalows the track winds up a gentle slope and enters a wood, full of singing birds in the spring, eventually coming out on Burning Cliff.

*In 1826 oil shales of the Kimmeridge Beds of the cliffs here burst into flames, continuing to burn for a year. They smouldered for a long time after that. The cause was the rapid oxidization of iron pyrites (*The Naturalist in Central Southern England, *see Bibliography).*

On reaching Burning Cliff there is a Coast Path sign. You keep to the top of the cliff-edge—along a 'cat-walk' at the start—which brings you in time to the top of White Nothe cliff.

At Burning Cliff there is also a path taking you down to the water's edge and on through the White Nothe landslip. This landslip path is only for the energetic and sure-footed; the last 200yds are up a fearsome gradient. This area, as with other landslips, is full of interest for the naturalist.

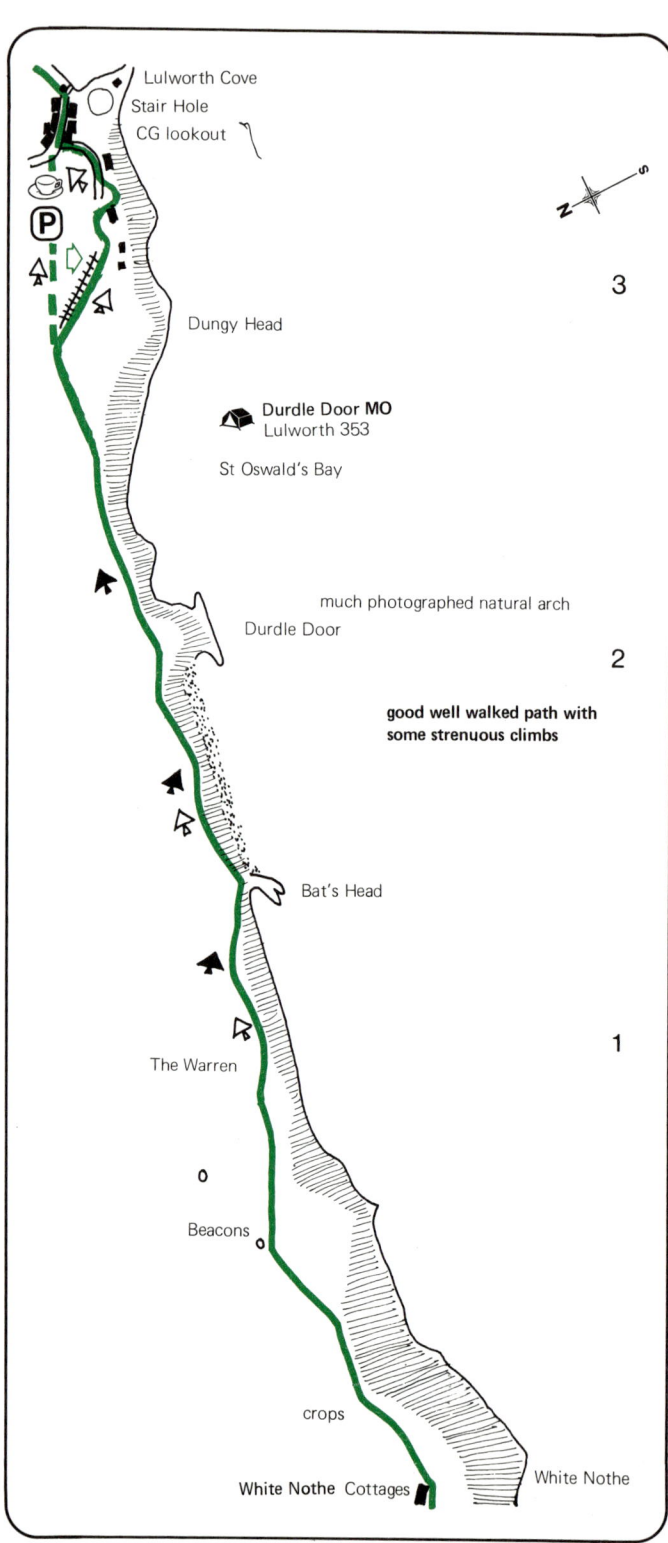

Lulworth Cove
Stair Hole
CG lookout

P

Dungy Head

Durdle Door MO
Lulworth 353

St Oswald's Bay

much photographed natural arch
Durdle Door

2

**good well walked path with
some strenuous climbs**

Bat's Head

1

The Warren

Beacons

crops

White Nothe Cottages

White Nothe

3

35 White Nothe-Lulworth Cove

3½ miles 5½km From Plymouth 154¼ miles 248¼km

Going: superb downland walking with some stiff ups and downs.

From White Nothe the Path keeps close to the edge of the cliff, rising to 500ft; turns a little inland to negotiate a small but steep combe; and continues, through the rolling downland, with three steep dips that need a lot of energy to climb out of.

From White Nothe you can see an obelisk to the left of the Path. This is a marker for ships at sea, a second obelisk is out of sight from the Path, behind the rise.

On the slopes of the next dip are the lines of early strip cultivation.

The small headland, Bat's Head, shows the chalk strata, with its lines of flint that have been under such pressure as to leave them vertical.

The next headland, Durdle Door, is of limestone which has proved more resistant than the chalk cliff behind it. The sea nevertheless has worn the much-photographed arch in the 200ft mass.

As you approach St Oswald's Bay and Dungy Head almost every step brings into view rock and cliff formations of intense interest. On the seaward side of the Path, just before you come to Lulworth Cove, is the Stair Hole. Here the sea has broken through the limestone and washed out a huge cave of which the roof has collapsed. The exposed limestone strata has been twisted into a figure S by titanic pressures millions of years ago.

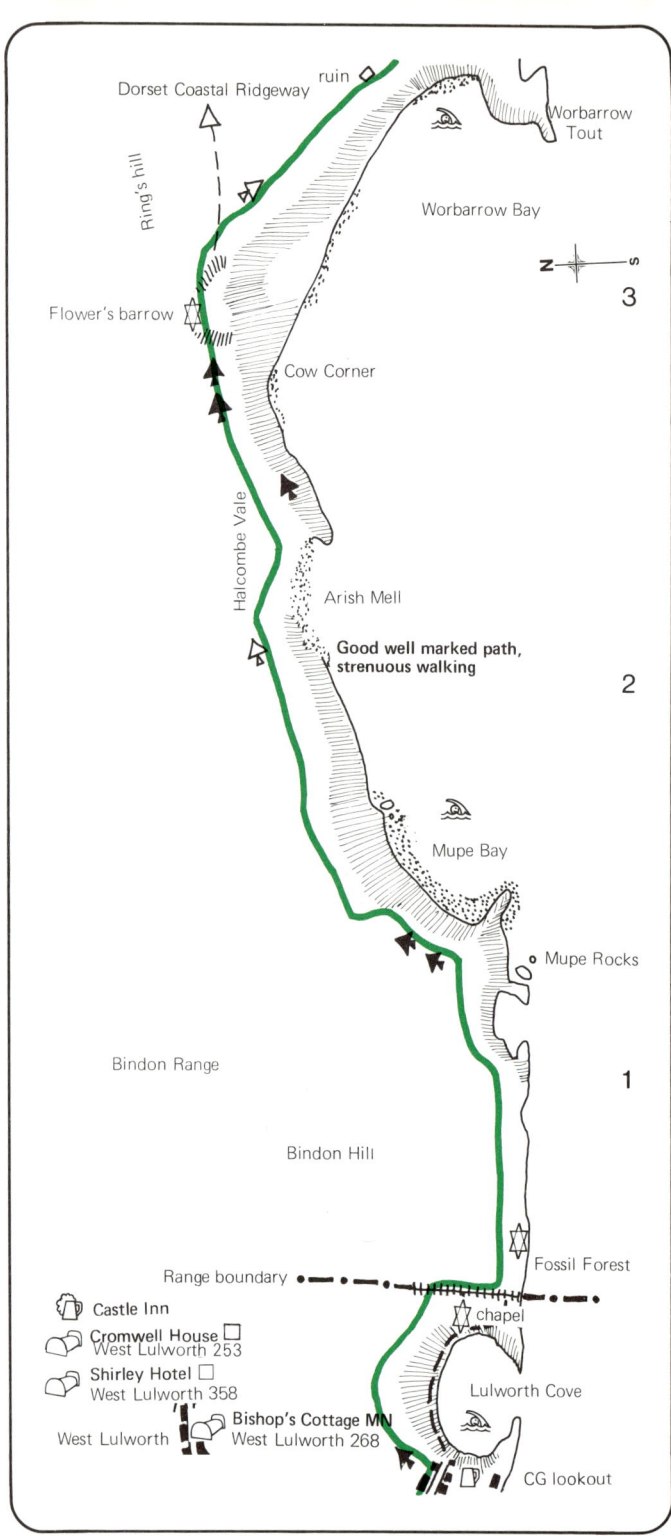

Dorset Coastal Ridgeway

ruin

Worbarrow Tout

Ring's hill

Worbarrow Bay

N ✦ S

3

Flower's barrow

Cow Corner

Halcombe Vale

Arish Mell

Good well marked path, strenuous walking

2

Mupe Bay

Mupe Rocks

Bindon Range

1

Bindon Hill

Range boundary

Fossil Forest

Castle Inn

chapel

Cromwell House
West Lulworth 253

Shirley Hotel
West Lulworth 358

Lulworth Cove

Bishop's Cottage M
West Lulworth 268

West Lulworth

CG lookout

36 Lulworth Cove-Worbarrow

3¾ miles 6km   From Plymouth 158 miles 254¼km

Going: as this section and the next (No. 37) are part of the Ministry of Defence Lulworth Ranges the most important question is whether the ranges are open or not. If you do manage to time your arrival aright you will find a most rewarding cliff walk, with stiff gradients.

The Ranges are open to the public every day in August and (roughly) the first two weeks in September. Additionally they are open for a week or more at Bank Holiday periods: Christmas, Easter, and the Spring Holiday, *plus* every Saturday and Sunday, with a few exceptions. It is as well to check on the position (unless you are walking in August) however. Write to: The Range Officer, RAC Gunnery School, Lulworth, Dorset; or phone Bindon Abbey 462721, Ext. 824.

If you arrive in Lulworth or Kimmeridge when the Range is closed you have to walk or hitch the 12 miles of road inland.

The Lulworth Ranges include about 7 miles of coastline, from Lulworth Cove to just west of Kimmeridge. The stretch is of particular attraction not only for its scenic beauty but also for its flora. There are no refreshment facilities.

Lulworth Cove is as popular with holidaymakers as with geologists. Here the sea has penetrated through a fault in the hard limestone and pushed back the softer clays and chalk of the cliff behind, making almost a perfect circular bay. Good bathing. All facilities for refreshment and accommodation; pub: the Cove Inn. All above facilities also in the charming village of West Lulworth, ½ mile inland; pub: the Castle.

To join the Coast Path you can either take the footpath along the 300ft cliff above the beach or walk along the beach and climb one of the tracks you will see going up to the top. On the cliff is the entrance to the Range Walks. **You must keep to the marked paths.** On your right (seawards) there are steps down to the Fossil Forest with many tufa-covered stumps of fossilized trees from the time of the Dinosaurs, 200 million years ago. You have quite a good view from the Path if you do not wish to climb down the steps. On the downs inland is the ruin of the 13th century chapel on the site of the original Bindon Abbey, moved to Wool in 1172. The Path continues over the springy turf of the cliff, with splendid views. It rounds Mupe Bay (bathing allowed when the Range is open) where the caves were used by smugglers, and climbs steeply before descending to Arish Mell (beach closed to public). The 17th-century Lulworth Castle can be seen 2 miles inland. Another long climb brings you to Flower's Barrow, with traces of a large Iron Age cliff fort dating from about 4th century BC.

The Barrow is the start of a very ancient Ridgeway going through to Corfe.

From Flowers Barrow a long steep descent leads to Worbarrow Bay (slippery in wet weather) where there is access to the long beach when the Range is open. Bathing permitted.

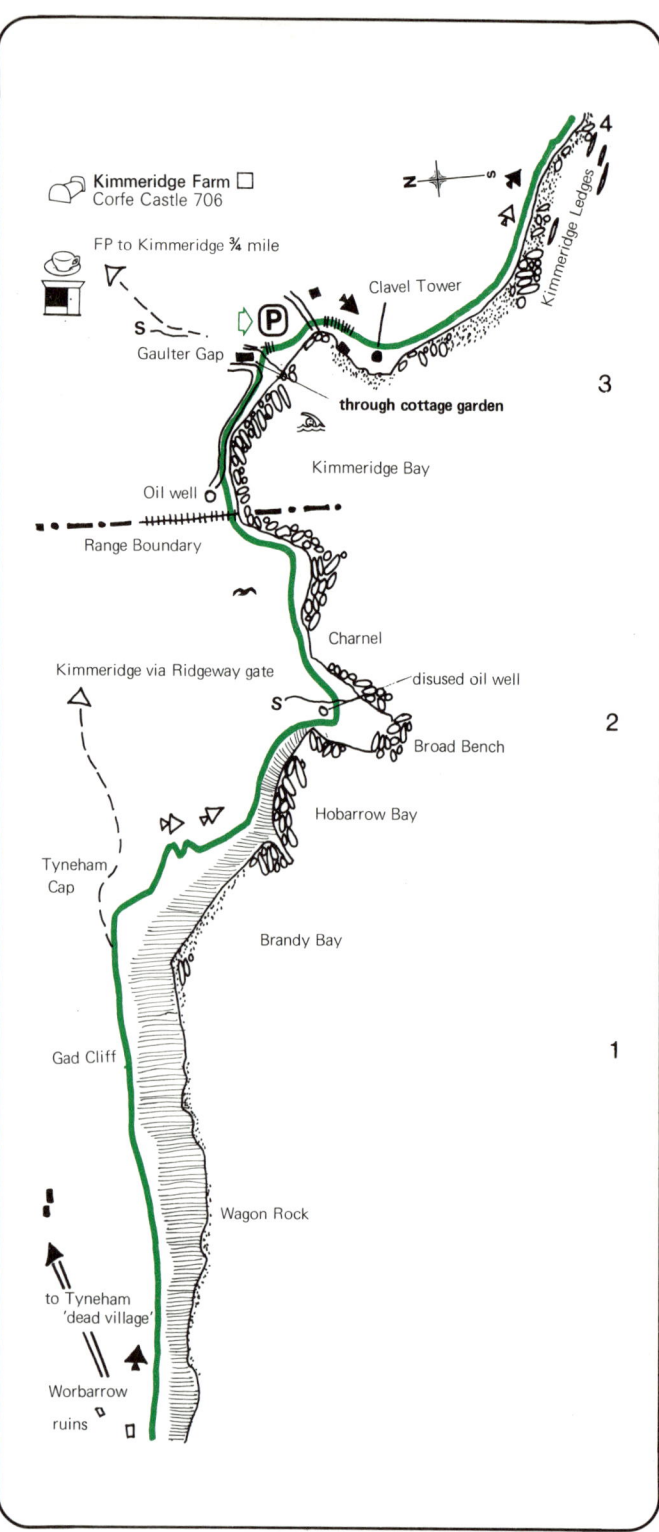

Kimmeridge Farm
Corfe Castle 706

FP to Kimmeridge ¾ mile

S

P

Gaulter Gap

Clavel Tower

through cottage garden

Kimmeridge Ledges

Kimmeridge Bay

Oil well

Range Boundary

Charnel

Kimmeridge via Ridgeway gate

S

disused oil well

Broad Bench

Hobarrow Bay

Tyneham Cap

Brandy Bay

Gad Cliff

Wagon Rock

to Tyneham
'dead village'

Worbarrow
ruins

4

3

2

1

37 Worbarrow-Kimmeridge Bay

4 miles 6½km   From Plymouth 162 miles 260¾km

Going: a good path along the cliffs. Still in the Range area but without the steep gradients of the first part (Section 36).

On the east side of Worbarrow Bay you have the promontory Worbarrow Tout (tout = look-out in Old English) on which you are allowed when the Range is open. An excellent vantage point for viewing this splendid part of the coast.

Inland, along a road 1¼ miles from Worbarrow is the 'dead' village of Tyneham which is of melancholy interest, its inhabitants having to leave in 1943 when the Army took over the area. On the slopes to the west of the road is the deserted farmstead of Baltington. When the Range is open there is a car park at Tyneham.

The Path climbs gradually from the disused Coast Guard station at Worbarrow to the top of Tyneham Cap (550ft). The cliff edge slopes inward so you have no sea views although those inland, over the rolling downland with patches of trees, are pleasant enough. From Tyneham Cap the Path descends, running round the edge of Hobarrow Bay, with the curious rock 'shelf' of Broad Bench, to Kimmeridge Bay.

You pass by Britain's most prolific inshore oil well, with its pump resembling in miniature the huge Cornish mining pumps of 200 years ago. It produces 400 barrels daily from the oil-bearing shales of the Kimmeridge Clays. The Range has quite a varied bird-life. Birds noted on a walk from Lulworth to Kimmeridge in late April include chaffinch, cormorant, herring gull, house martin, jackdaw, kestrel, rock pipit, skylark, stonechat, swallow, and wheatear. A cuckoo and a blackcap were also heard. Wild flowers: bluebell, cowslip, wild cabbage and early purple orchid. There are reputedly many other kinds of wild flower, including some rarities, so watch where you step. Also butterflies, but you would be lucky indeed to see the rare small brown and black Lulworth skipper, first seen at Lulworth some years ago.

A short way up the road by the former Coast Guard cottages brings you to Kimmeridge (1 mile), or there is a footpath leading off on the left of the road which takes you across fields to the village. You can get tea and refreshments at the post office.

The Coast Path will be seen leading down the seaward side of the old Coast Guard cottages, round the curve of the beach of Gaulter Gap (now a favourite for skin diving) and up some steps, to help you reach the top of the cliff where there is a ruined folly, the Clavel Tower, built in 1800 by the Reverend Clavel who used it as an observatory.

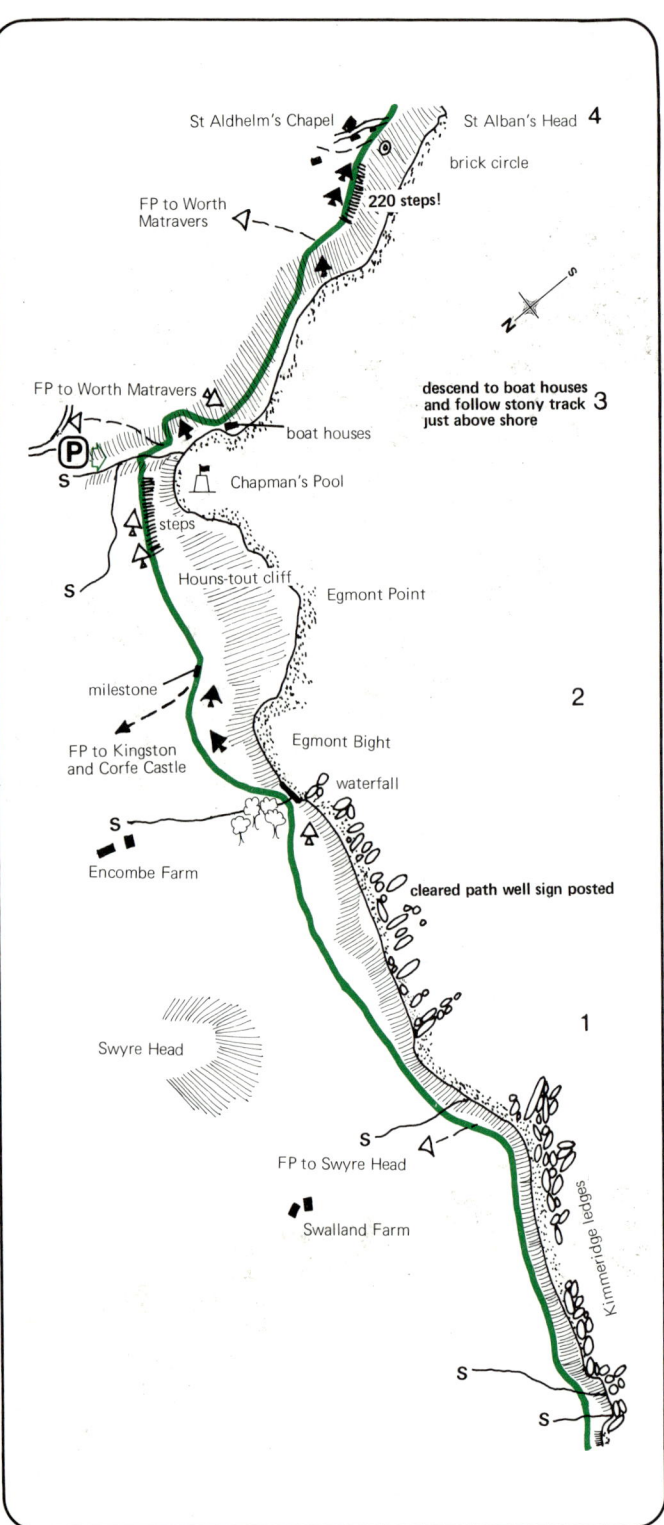

St Aldhelm's Chapel

St Alban's Head **4**

brick circle

220 steps!

FP to Worth
Matravers

FP to Worth Matravers

**descend to boat houses
and follow stony track 3
just above shore**

P

S

boat houses

Chapman's Pool

steps

Houns-tout cliff

Egmont Point

2

milestone

FP to Kingston
and Corfe Castle

Egmont Bight

waterfall

S

cleared path well sign posted

Encombe Farm

Swyre Head

1

FP to Swyre Head

S

Swalland Farm

Kimmeridge ledges

S

S

38 Kimmeridge Bay-St Alban's Head

4 miles 6½km   From Plymouth 166 miles 267¼km
Going: good cliff walking, with two steep climbs although
steps have been cut on one of them to help!

From the Clavel Tower the Coast Path continues along the
cliff top past cultivated fields; below you is the beach and the
rocky 'spines' of the Kimmeridge Ledges.

The Path drops down to Egmont Bight where the stream,
emerging from some private woods, tumbles over the cliff edge
in a small waterfall. There is a stiff gradient up Houns-tout
Cliff and down the other side to Chapman's Pool (steps
provided; a great help if you are coming in the other direction).

*Chapman's Pool is a relatively quiet, pebble and sand beach.
Swimming when the sea is calm. No facilities for refreshment. A
favourite spot for fossil hunters.*

At the back of the beach, by a footbridge over the small
stream, there is a stone marker indicating the direction of the
Path down through the rocky, gorse-covered valley. Head for
the beach. If tide is right walk on beach round to boathouses.
If tide is in take a left turn and then right. This takes you above
the beach and down to the boathouses. The Path continues
close to the shore eventually veering inland to the 220 steps to
the top of St Alban's Head.

*On St Alban's (or St Aldhelm's) Head is St Aldhelm's
Chapel, dedicated to the first Bishop of Sherborne (AD 705),
and thought to have been built between 1150 and 1200. It may
have been intended more for a guide to shipping as the centre
turret could have held a lantern (the cross is modern). It is quite
square with walls 3¼ft thick. The roof is supported by a pillar
with four stone arches, which is unusual.*

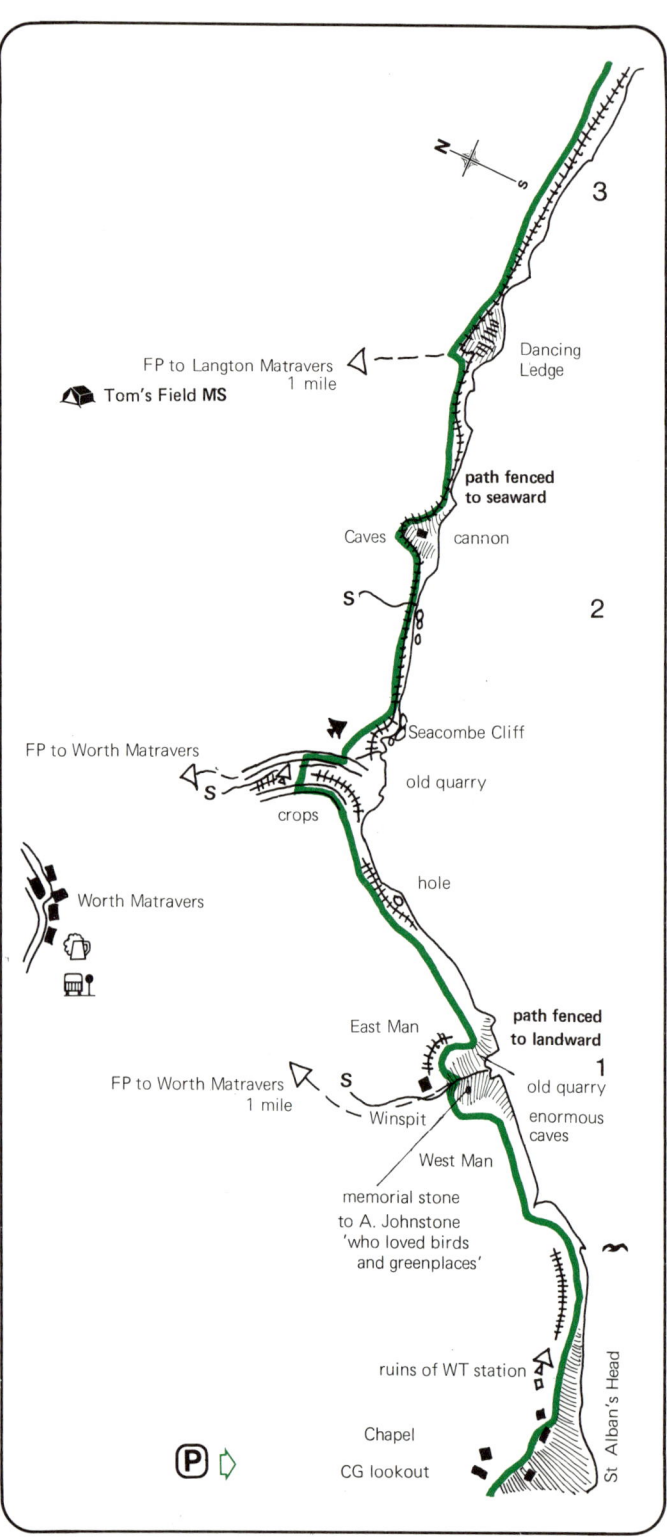

N

3

FP to Langton Matravers
1 mile

Tom's Field MS

Dancing
Ledge

path fenced
to seaward

Caves
cannon

S

2

FP to Worth Matravers

Seacombe Cliff

S

old quarry

crops

hole

Worth Matravers

East Man

path fenced
to landward

1

FP to Worth Matravers
1 mile

S

old quarry

enormous
caves

Winspit

West Man

memorial stone
to A. Johnstone
'who loved birds
and greenplaces'

ruins of WT station

St Alban's Head

Chapel

CG lookout

P

39 St Alban's Head-Dancing Ledge

3¼ miles 5¼km From Plymouth 169¼ miles 272½km
Going: beautiful cliff-top walking on a clear, slightly undulating Path.

From the Chapel on St Alban's Head a stone marker shows the Path proceeding east along the cliff, past the Coast Guard lookout and the remains of some wartime WT (Wireless Telegraph) installations.

A line running from St Alban's Head north-west to Wareham is the west boundary of what is known as the Isle of Purbeck. It is in no way an island but really the south-east corner of Dorset; in earlier days it was rather isolated by high ground and marsh.

The Path runs close to the cliff edge (besides the ever-present herring gulls there are fulmars, kittiwakes, guillemots, and razorbills to be seen on the cliff).

After about 1 mile you come to the disused quarries at Winspit.

The Winspit area provides an example of the variety of the wild life on the coast. The spider-orchid is found here and recently the very rare bird, the wall-creeper, wintered on the cliffs. From Winspit there is a track inland to Worth Matravers, a charming village with thatched houses, a fine Norman church, and a good pub—the Square and Compass, patronized by Augustus John, apparently, from the sketch he has left behind. The Square and Compass are the stone-mason's equipment—the local quarries provided the purbeck marble for the pillars of Salisbury Cathedral in the 13th century. There is a good bus service to Swanage.

Farther on past Seacombe Cliff (another path leads from here to Worth Matravers), down on a rocky ledge, there is an old cannon, giving the name Cannon Cove. You then come to Dancing Ledge, used for shipping stone from the quarries; it has a swimming pool cut in the rock—an idea of a local schoolmaster for his boys.

In January 1786 the East Indiaman Halsewell *was wrecked off Seacombe cliff. 168 were drowned including the captain and his two daughters. 80 were saved by the local people who hauled them up the cliff.*

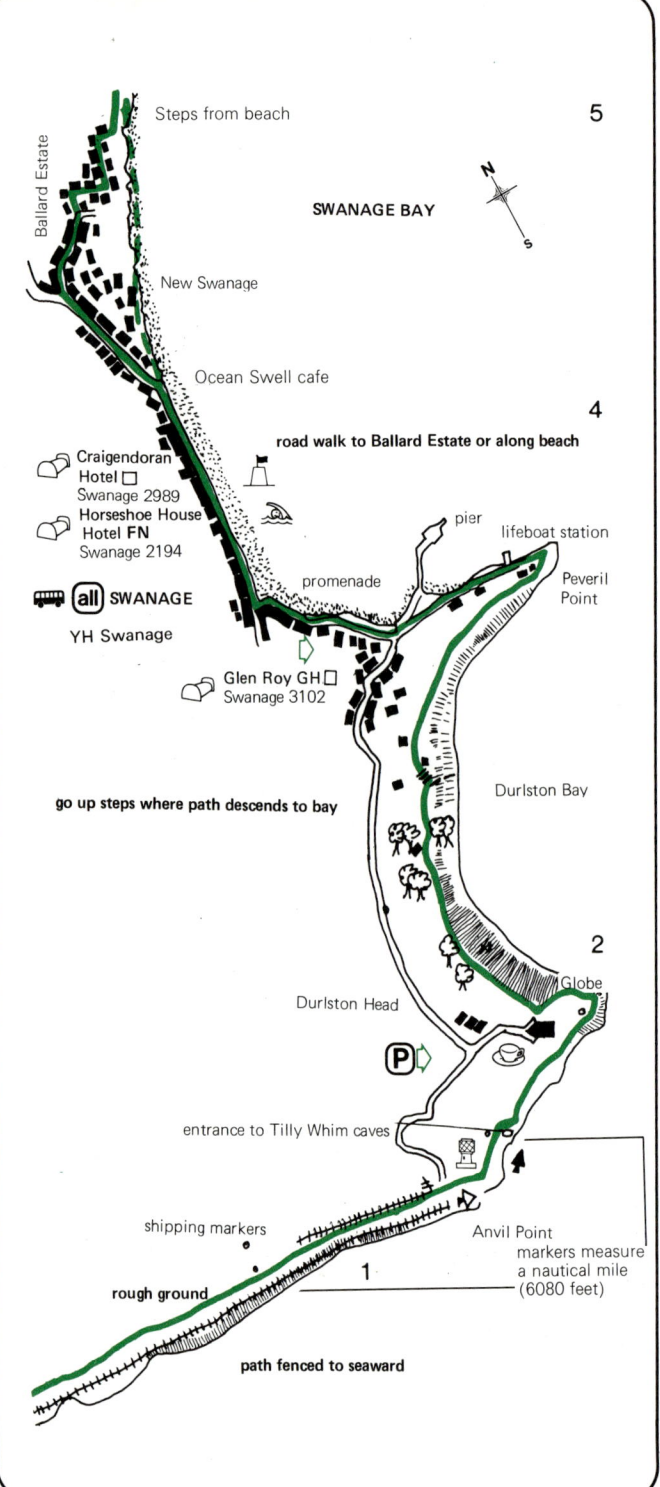

Steps from beach

5

Ballard Estate

SWANAGE BAY

New Swanage

N

S

Ocean Swell cafe

4

road walk to Ballard Estate or along beach

Craigendoran
Hotel ☐
Swanage 2989

Horseshoe House
Hotel **FN**
Swanage 2194

pier

lifeboat station

Peveril
Point

🚌 **all** SWANAGE

promenade

YH Swanage

Durlston Bay

Glen Roy GH☐
Swanage 3102

go up steps where path descends to bay

2

Globe

Durlston Head

Ⓟ

entrance to Tilly Whim caves

shipping markers

Anvil Point

markers measure
a nautical mile
(6080 feet)

rough ground

1

path fenced to seaward

88

40 Dancing Ledge-Swanage

5 miles 8km   From Plymouth 174¼ miles 280½km
Going: continuing on a good cliff path with some points of interest on nearing Swanage.

From above Dancing Ledge the Path proceeds through mainly pastureland until Anvil Point is reached.

The lighthouse, built in 1881, can be visited on weekday afternoons.

A short distance farther on are the much-visited Tilly Whim Caves which are in fact disused stone quarries ('whim' is a hoist or crane in local dialect, and Tilly was the owner).

The mile of cliff between Durlston Head and Peveril Point is of geological interest as it shows all the three formations of what is known as Purbeck Beds. A rock from the area was found with the imprint of the foot of a prehistoric Iguanadon. It can be seen in the British Museum.

On Durlston Head is Durlston Castle, a Victorian house, now a restaurant, and a large stone globe of the world.

As you round Peveril Point there is a fine view of Poole Bay and the town of Swanage.

Swanage (population: 8500): mentioned in the Domesday Book, it has a place in history as the scene of a sea battle in the 9th century when Alfred's Saxons routed the Danish fleet in Swanage Bay. Those Danish ships that survived the battle became wrecked farther down the coast. The small village living by its fishing and stone quarries became a popular resort with the coming of the railway. Good sandy beach and all facilities for the holidaymaker.

The official route of the Coast Path is along the Front (Shore Road) of Swanage then inland, up the main road (Upwell Road) for ½ mile, then down Ballard Way—on the right near the roundabout—to the Ballard Estate, a collection of bungalows. Walk through the Estate and you come to a Coast Path sign leading out onto the cliff. Most people will prefer the shorter and more pleasant way by walking along the beach. Just past the last wooden breakwater there is a short footpath leading from the sands up the low cliff and the Coast Path.

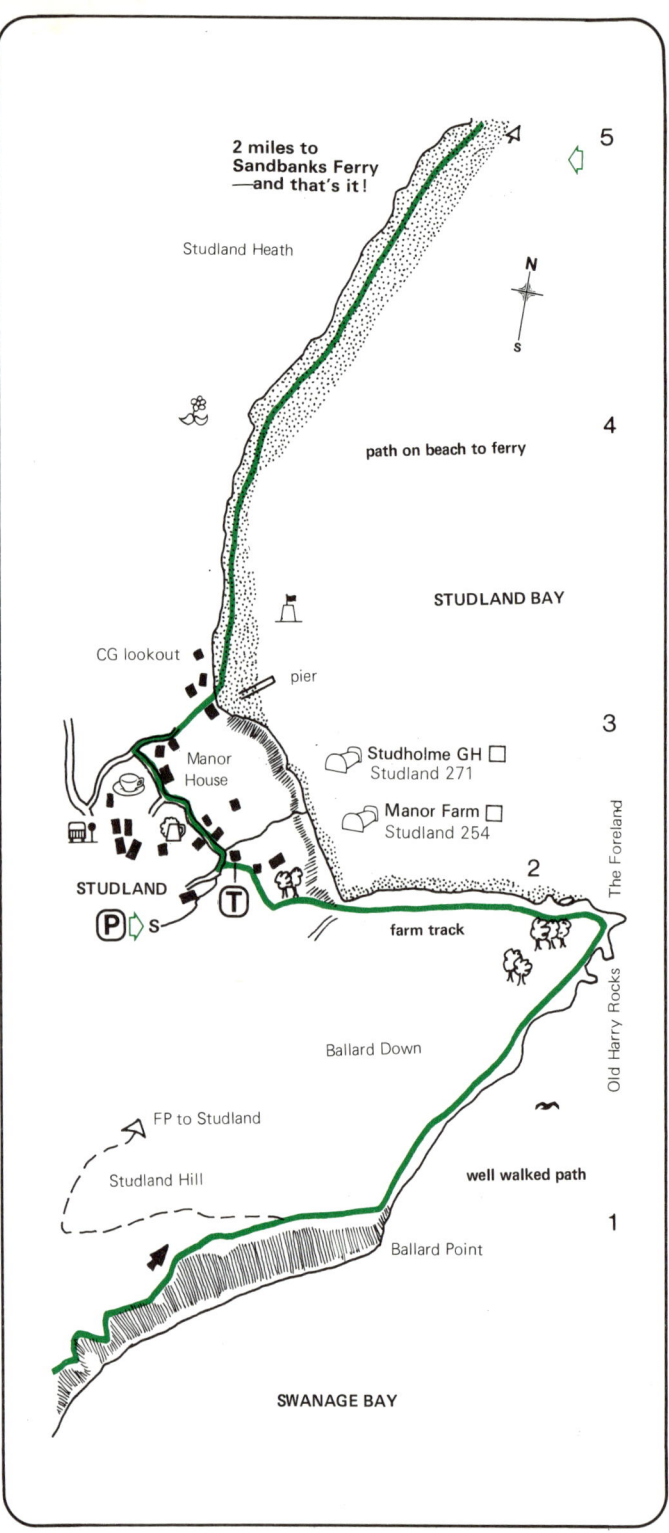

2 miles to
Sandbanks Ferry
—and that's it!

Studland Heath

N

S

CG lookout

pier

path on beach to ferry

STUDLAND BAY

Manor
House

Studholme GH
Studland 271

Manor Farm
Studland 254

STUDLAND

The Foreland

P ◁ S

T

farm track

Ballard Down

FP to Studland

Studland Hill

well walked path

Old Harry Rocks

Ballard Point

SWANAGE BAY

41 Swanage-South Haven Point (Bournemouth)

6½ miles 10½km From Plymouth 180¾ miles 291km

Going: these last few miles of the South-west Peninsula Coast Path have good variety: 2 miles of high-cliff walking with fine views; a charming village and a Nature Reserve.

You emerge on Ballard Down, a fine stretch of open downland. Birds to be seen in spring include chiffchaff, whitethroat, linnet, stonechat, corn bunting, and skylark.

As you come round Ballard Down the yellow-brown cliffs of the Swanage area give way to chalk and ahead is The Foreland with its famous chalk pillars of Old Harry and Old Harry's Wife.

The Path then turns west and after 1 mile comes out on the road at Studland, one of the best-known Dorset beauty spots.

The Church of St Nicholas is almost purely Norman but incorporates one or two Saxon features. Both unusual and amusing are the exterior carvings of faces, animal's heads, etc, just below the eaves of the roof. These are Norman. The churchyard has the grave of Sgt. Lawrence who came through all the Napoleonic campaigns, married a French girl, and took a pub in the village. Village pub: the Bankes Arms. There is a bus service to Swanage and Bournemouth.

A short step beyond the church the road leads down to the sandy beach. A Coast Path sign points in the direction of the sandhills behind the 3½ mile long sandy bay but the route is far from clear; it is better to keep to the beach and the firm sands.

The whole of Studland Heath, ie the area fringing the shore, is a 400-acre Nature Reserve with flora and fauna of great variety. There is a Nature Trail in the Reserve. The entrance is at Knoll House, 1 mile up the road from Studland to South Haven Point.

The Coast Path finishes unobtrusively after the 3½ miles along the sands of Studland Bay, at South Haven Point where the ferry runs every 10 minutes to Sandbanks (Bournemouth) except during two weeks in November.

If you are walking east-west and plan to walk from Kimmeridge to Lulworth, check if the Path is open as it is an army range (see Sections 36 and 37).

Walking in the Torbay area (Brixham, Paignton, Torquay)

In 1968 Torquay, Paignton, and Brixham were amalgamated to form Devon's largest holiday resort, Torbay, extending for almost 20 miles of coast, with a resident population of over 100,000.

The official Coast Path from Brixham finishes after 2 miles at Goodrington (Paignton). On the other side of Torquay, from above the Harbour, there are number of cliff paths with fine views.

You can if you wish travel right through Torquay from Goodrington to Babbacombe (Oddicombe). The bus runs via Paignton and the centre of Torquay. If you prefer to walk as far as you can on paths without much road walking here are the details. (There is a helpful booklet *Torbay Coast Paths*, 50p, from local bookshops.)

From Fishcombe Road, Brixham, (Section 14) take the Path which leads steeply down through woods towards the sea. After rather a scramble you will come out to the delightful Churston Cove. You climb out of Churston Cove by a steep narrow zig-zag path over the rocks which brings you, through woods, along the fence of the Churston Golf Course for about 1 mile. You then emerge from the woods above Elberry Cove. Walk along the beach, following the curve of Broad Sands Beach, mainly pebbles. The Path then turns inland to cross the Torbay Steam Railway (see Section 13) and runs along the side of the line as far as Goodrington. Distance from Fishcombe Road 2½ miles.

East of Torquay there are paths just east of the harbour, then skirting Meadfoot Beach and taking Marine Drive you come to the spectacular Hope's Nose by a path. Off the Nose are the islands: Thatcher's Rock, Ore Stone, and Flat Rock, the last-named being the home of hundreds of gulls—it has the largest breeding colony of kittiwakes in Devon.

Rejoining Marine Drive a wooded path, Bishop's Walk, leads round Black Head and Anstey's Cove back to the road. A few yards on the road and a path runs round Long Quarry Point and down into Babbacombe Beach with its tiny pier. There is a good pub, the Fishermen's Arms. The Path continues just above the beach level and starts climbing near the lower station of the Cliff Railway on Oddicombe beach.

The whole distance from the harbour is about 3½ miles.

Plymouth

Plymouth (population 252,000): famous city and naval port, grew from the little Sutton Harbour near the centre of the present city. In 1250 the priors of nearby Plympton took over the harbour, naming it Plymouth. Sited at the mouth of two rivers, the Tamar and the Plym, with its magnificent anchorage in the bay—Plymouth Sound, it grew in importance as a military port in the Middle Ages during the wars with France, with whom it also traded. As the home of Hawkins and Drake, Plymouth became the main base for the war with Spain in the 16th century and the fleet sailed from here against the Armada.

It was in June 1620 that the *Speedwell*, taking the Pilgrim Fathers to America, limped into Plymouth with a leak and transferred her 102 passengers to the *Mayflower* which completed the historic voyage, commemorated by a monument.

In the 17th century fortifications and the large naval dockyard at Devonport were built. The next two centuries saw further growth in both naval and commercial activity, but the centre of the city suffered immense destruction from air raids in August 1941. This has been rebuilt and Plymouth is now not only a thriving industrial city and port but also a major resort. Most of the big yacht races start from here. Of special interest are the

16th-century houses in New Street near Sutton Harbour, and the old Barbican.

Useful addresses: Bus station, Breton Side (near Civic Centre) (bus enquiries: Plymouth 68000); Head Post Office, St Andrews Cross (near Civic Centre); Information Centre, Civic Centre (Plymouth 68000. Exts 2309 and 2409).

Torquay

Torquay before the 19th century was only a small Devon hamlet. The monks of Torre Abbey, founded in the 12th century, had been responsible for building the first small harbour where the present one stands. During the Napoleonic Wars (1796-1815) the British fleet spent much time anchored in Tor Bay and the officers, recognizing the beauty and mild climate of Torquay, installed their wives and families there. Helped by the arrival of the railway in 1848, Torquay grew further and prospered.

Places of interest: *Kent's Cavern* (see Historical Note).

Torre Abbey Parts of the old Abbey still remain, including the Gatehouse, and the 16th-century house, in pleasant gardens.

Cockington An old 16th-century village, preserved on the west outskirts of Torquay.

Torquay and Paignton (adjoining on the south) have 19 beaches to choose from.

Addresses in Torquay and Paignton
Torquay Information Bureau, 9, Vaughan Parade (Inner Harbour) (Phone 27428); General Post Office, Fleet Street (near The Strand); Police Station, South Street.

Paignton Information Bureau, Eastern Esplanade (Phone 58383); General Post Office, Palace Avenue.

In Torquay, The Strand, just above the Inner Harbour, could be called the centre of the resort. Most local bus services start or call there.

Weymouth

For the route by footpath into Weymouth (Section 32) continue along the Fleet, past a caravan site at the head of a small bay and then up along the seaward boundary of a field. A short diversion takes you round a Defence area, and after about 1 mile, through a caravan site and down to the main road crossing the Ferry Bridge to Portland (you can get a bus from here to Weymouth if you wish).

Cross the main road opposite the Royal Victoria pub and there is a path along a factory fence. This follows the shore of Portland Harbour and then takes to a road, past the ruins of Sandfoot Castle, built by Henry VIII. At the dip in the road you enter on the right the Undercliff Walk through trees and flowering shrubs, emerging into Nothe Gardens above Weymouth Harbour. You can cross the short width of the harbour by ferry in the summer or walk to the Town Bridge along the Quay, with its charming bow-windowed houses and old pubs every few yards.

The Romans had a port at nearby Radipole. In the early Middle Ages two small villages grew on each side of the Wey, Weymouth and Melcombe Regis, that were raided twice by the French in the 1300's. In 1348 refugees from the Continent trying to escape the Black Death landed at Melcombe Regis and brought the Plague with them, which slew perhaps one third of England's population. Weymouth survived the 15th and 16th century, Queen Elizabeth ordering the two rival villages to join. George III spent much time at Weymouth, 1789-1805. Radipole Lake, behind the east side of the town, is a bird sanctuary. The Coast Path does not include the Isle of Portland, reached by the road from Ferry Bridge. Source of the famous Portland stone it is also noted for its flora and fauna.

Historical Note

The most fascinating archaeological site on the Path between Plymouth and Poole Harbour is Kent's Cavern in Torquay. This large limestone cave was found on excavation to contain traces of human habitation from Palaeolithic (Old Stone Age) of more than 12,000 years ago: hand-axes antler harpoons, needles, etc. Bones of mammals included mammoth, sabre-toothed tiger, grizzly bear, and horse—specimen finds are in the Torquay museum. There is only one other site in Britain which has produced evidence of similar ancient origin.

The coast covered in this book is divided between Devon and Dorset. The two counties stem from the territories of the Dumnonii and the Durotriges, two Celtic tribes who arrived from north France in the 1st century BC. The Romans subsequently ruled the Dumnonii from Exeter and the Durotriges from Dorchester (Durnovaria). The division of the land survived both the departure of the Romans, and the Dark Ages, with the Saxons who followed laying the foundations of the counties as we know them. On the Path near Lulworth, the Bindon Hill earthwork is reckoned to be a defensive foothold of some Celtic tribe a short time before the Durotriges arrived.

Devon and Dorset became part of the Saxon kingdom of Wessex between 500 and 800, although Devon was one of the last areas to be conquered. The Saxons became gradually converted to Christianity, and in Dorset the first bishop of Sherborne, St Aldhelm, was consecrated in 708. Although Alfred later successfully defended Wessex against the Danes, scattering their fleet off Swanage in 877, the Danes conquered 100 years later. The men of Devon and Dorset had been able to withstand a number of earlier Danish raids. The Danish King Canute's seneschal founded Abbotsbury Abbey in 1026.

The Normans in turn subdued the country and seem not to have met much opposition in Devon and Dorset. The Anglo-Norman kings re-organized the country, and depended on the coastal towns for ships and men for their campaigns in France. The Dissolution of the Monasteries in the 16th century transformed land-ownership, the leading families taking over the large estates. The power and position of the wealthy abbeys may be gauged by the traces of their buildings still remaining in Abbotsbury.

In Elizabethan times Plymouth and Dartmouth played a dominant part in the war with Spain. The changeover to Protestantism took place without undue fuss.

In the Civil War Devon and Dorset were mainly on the side of Parliament but many towns and villages changed hands in the fighting. Later, a strong Puritan element emerged and families from Plymouth, Weymouth, and places near emigrated to practise their faith without interference and to help found the present America.

Agriculture has always been the means of livelihood in Devon and Dorset, with fishing on the coast; in the 18th and 19th century fishing was supplemented by smuggling. The lonely coast behind Chesil Beach was a favourite spot for landing contraband. Stone quarrying also helped in Dorset, and in the mid-1800's the railways brought holidaymakers to the sandy beaches and cliffs, founding the present important tourist industry.

Geology, Flowers, Birds

The coast east of Plymouth is composed of Devonian sandstones and shales which give way as you go east to earlier sandstones, limestones, clays and chalk, or a mixture of these. They range in age from 350 to 70 million years. The characteristic red cliffs and soil for some distance east of Torquay are a later iron-stained sandstone which was formed in desert conditions, giving it the 'burnt' appearance. Of particular interest on this sector are the landslip areas of which the one between Seaton and Lyme Regis is the best-known. This and other areas of geological, botanical, and bird interest are mentioned below.

On the Path you again come across raised beaches as on the stretches of the Path dealt with in the other books in this series. Just east of Prawle Point and east of Teignmouth, for example, the beach has been raised some feet and the sea-cliffs are now some distance inland. One theory is that the beach level sprang back after being relieved of the weight of the ice of the Ice Age.

Beer Head

The high chalk cliffs make a superb vantage point for bird-watching, particularly in the autumn: gannets off-shore, also kittiwakes, lesser black-backed gulls, shearwaters, terns, and the occasional skua; there are land migrations of wagtails, meadow pipits and tree pipits. Species that may be observed during autumn migration include chiffchaff, blackcap, willow warbler, spotted flycatcher, redstart, lesser whitethroat, ring ouzel, sedge warbler, and pied flycatcher.

The vegetation is in strong contrast to that of the rest of the Devon coast. Gone is the heather, bracken, and gorse which will by now be so familiar to the walker. It is replaced by short turf with shrubs such as wild privet, hawthorn, and dogwood, with also wayfaring tree and scrambling old man's beard showing the presence of lime in the soil. Look out for mullion and nodding thistle.

Slapton Lye

This is the largest freshwater area in the British Isles so close to the sea, covering 248 acres. Water is impounded by a shingle ridge as at Loe Bar (see Book 2 *From St Ives to Plymouth*), and Swanpool at Falmouth. Sixty per cent of the shingle is composed of flint. The Lye and the shingle ridge form part of a Nature Reserve. There are excellent shore and aquatic plants. The area is on the main line of coastal bird migration, and the Lye attracts wintering fowl. A large coot population is found here; reed warblers are common.

Lulworth Cove and Range

At Lulworth Cove the sea has broken through the resistant limestone and eaten into the softer Wealden Clay behind. A similar feature but smaller is the adjacent Stair Hole, also the larger Mupe and Worbarrow Bays to the east (Lulworth Range). Lulworth Ranges, used by the Army (see Sections 36 and 37), have a variety of flower and plant life because human access has been limited. The Ranges are now open more frequently than in the past, and the Coast Path runs through them.

Axmouth to Lyme Regis Undercliffs

This landslip area is a Nature Reserve. Of great interest geologically, cliffs composed of chalk with sandstone and clays beneath have collapsed exposing fossil-bearing limestone, and creating an unusual vegetation including a natural growing ash wood (see Section 24).

Dawlish Warren Sand Dunes

Flora includes the interesting maritime species zostera or eel grass, also fenugreek, soft and suffocating clover, chaffweed, flax seed, glasswort on the mud, and two interesting grasses—giant quaking grass and harestail. Sand crocuses are also to be found.

Bibliography

Automobile Association *Book of the Seaside*, 1972
Burrows R *The Naturalist in Devon and Cornwall*, 1971
Dyer J *Southern England. An Archaeological Guide*, 1973
Fox A *South-West England 3500* BC-AD *600*, 1973
Hoskins W G *Devon*, 1974
National Trust *The National Trust Guide*, 1973
Knowlton D *The Naturalist in Central Southern England*, 1973
Seymour J *The Companion Guide to the Coast of South-West England*, 1974
South-West Way Association *Annual Reports*
Better Pubs, Red Cross House, Crediton, Devon publish map-guides to pubs in east and west Cornwall, south and east Devon, Dorset and Somerset.

Acknowledgments

Help has been received from many kind people in compiling this book and this the authors gratefully acknowledge. They would particularly like to mention Roger Burrows, BA, MI Biol, of Exeter University, for his advice and help over flora, wild life, and geology; Roger Butts of the Cornwall Members' Group of the Royal Society for the Protection of Birds for help on birds; the Countryside Commission, Cheltenham, and HM Coastguard at Wyke Regis.

Anyone walking the Path soon becomes aware of the sterling work done by the National Trust in keeping the area accessible for everyone.

The South-west Way Association is dedicated to furthering the interests of walkers of the South-west Peninsula Coast Path, acting as a watch-dog where access to the Path is threatened and prodding lethargic local authorities into observing their legal responsibility to make available and maintain the section of the Path in their territories. Members are kept informed by regular reports of all matters concerning the Path. Details from Kynance, 15, Old Newton Road, Kingskerswell, Newton Abbot, Devon.

The authors gratefully acknowledge the ready assistance given by the Honorary Secretary Mr Phil Carter.

Many sources have been used including the works listed in the Bibliography. Every care has been taken but conditions are so liable to change that the publishers can assume no responsibility for any inaccuracies.